AN EXPERIMENT IN EDUCATION

AN EXPERIMENT IN EDUCATION

BY

SYBIL MARSHALL

CAMBRIDGE
AT THE UNIVERSITY PRESS
1963

PUBLISHED BY

THE SYNDICS OF THE CAMBRIDGE UNIVERSITY PRESS

Bentley House, 200 Euston Road, London, N.W. 1
American Branch: 32 East 57th Street, New York 22, N.Y.
West African Office: P.O. Box 33, Ibadan, Nigeria

CAMBRIDGE UNIVERSITY PRESS

1963

First printed 1963
Reprinted 1963

Printed in Great Britain at the University Press, Cambridge
(Brooke Crutchley, University Printer)

To all my children

CONTENTS

The publishers and author are grateful to Children's Play Activities Ltd, for a generous grant which made possible the inclusion of the coloured plates. Children's Play Activities is an educational charity which aims to promote the understanding of children's play and the proper provision of play-time, play-space and play-things. The grant was made because in the view of C.P.A., this book illustrates how the dynamic of play-situations may be used to inspire educational activity of the highest order.

⤛ 1 ⤜

As Confucius said, a journey of a thousand miles begins with one step; but it is an unfortunate traveller who discovers after the first two hundred miles or so that he has been going in the wrong direction.

My journey into the world of art in general, and into children's art in particular, began in that way. If I heard the word 'art' at all in my childhood, it had no connection in my mind with the lesson called 'drawing' on the school timetable. Sometimes on a Sunday evening, as we walked in family groups to chapel, my father would stop to admire a field more than usually well 'stouked', or a cluster of newly thatched cornstacks, or potato stetches straight as ribbing on a piece of knitting, and remark 'Ah. That's h'art, that is'.

Or again, in October, we would be taking the same walk in the early evening as the sun began to set. Then the blue and white pudding-basin under which we walked would turn suddenly into the gayest of rainbow-coloured sunshades, with even its most easterly rim made of pink chiffon. The black, gold and green checks of the flat fenland tablecloth would be divided by stripes of pale yellow or gleaming orange, where-ever dykes and drains threw back the colour to the sky. There was only one spot in the whole scene where the rim of the sky could not actually be seen to rest upon the earth, and that was due west, where a mile-long row of poplar trees cut off the horizon from view, and it was exactly there that the sun would finally plunge out of sight. Then my mother would gaze and gaze at the fret-work of tall black trees against the crimson sky and say, 'Somebody ought to paint that'.

Somebody ought, indeed; but there have been few painters who could do justice to a fenland sunset in October. A Turner, a Constable and a Matthew Smith rolled into one, born and bred in the fens, might perhaps have attempted it; but I doubt if even he would have succeeded in capturing more than a reflected reflection of that glory.

The Thursday afternoon drawing lessons, however, had nothing to do with all this. Every Thursday, after we had sung 'Be present at our table, Lord', our teacher said, 'Eyes open. Hands down. Don't forget to bring something to draw.'

I lived only a hundred yards from the school, and the dinner-time of an hour and a half was long enough for food and for play in the farmyard as well. When, at 1.25 p.m., my face had been hastily wiped and my jumper divested of loose straws and 'sweethearts', I would remember the 'something to draw'. On each side of the garden path, just inside our front gate, a laurel bush grew. On Thursday after Thursday after Thursday, I clawed a spray of leaves from one or the other of them, and as the bell began to ring I ran towards school pulling off the leathery leaves and dropping them behind me like Hansel and Gretel's peas, till I stood panting in 'the line', clutching in my hand a long, pale green stalk, at the top of which still remained two forlorn but symmetrically opposite lateral leaves. Sometimes I yielded to tearful entreaties of 'Give us a leaf', and arrived at my desk in class with only one.

Then out from a cupboard came our drawing books, white cartridge paper in green covers, about 11 by 7 inches, our H.B. pencils sharpened to a needle point, and an india-rubber. In my heavy, hot, tensed hand, the pencil became a graving tool, scoring deep through many pages. No rubber could ever erase the marks it left on the top page. A wetted finger sometimes helped, and even a tear or two came in useful, until the resistance of the paper at last gave way, and a hole appeared in the sketched leaf which Nature had neglected to arrange in the original. As the sketch was usually no more than a quarter of the natural size, the hole sometimes accounted for most of the drawing, and there was very little left to show if teacher wanted to see it.

Sometimes the routine varied and we were given the tea-pot, the coal scuttle, the handbell or a pair of tongs to draw. On those days I suffered acutely, for I had not then the experience of previous Thursdays to rely upon to help me through.

Our teacher was in no way to blame for the conditions I have described. She was an excellent teacher, who taught me things of much greater value than ever could be found in a text-book. It was from her I first learned that one cannot justify one's existence in a small community if one is not prepared to be of it. She also made me understand that from those to whom much is given, much is expected; and that most doors will open to those who have courage to knock. She did no worse than her colleagues in the matter of 'art', either. If anything, she did better, for she seemed to sense the need for something different, even while following the usual routine, and without knowing at all where to begin to break it. When 'the New Art' was beginning to be heard of even in districts as remote as ours, she at least gave it a trial with the means immediately at her disposal. I remember the occasion well. We were told one day to divide our drawing page into four, using a ruler. Having done so, we put down our pencils and folded our arms while teacher explained that today we were to tell a story in four pictures, one in each rectangle on the page we had just prepared. I had been brought up on the books and illustrations of Louis Wain, and my imaginative world had always been peopled with cats. I seized my pencil and began, while scene after scene of my story flashed upon the screen of my imagination. My four pictures told the story of a family of cats, complete with portmanteaux, making a journey by train from our local station to Yarmouth, where herrings hung in rows to welcome them.

I do not suppose for one moment that anyone other than I could possibly have recognised the creatures I drew, nor have interpreted their story; but in my mind's eye they still make their smoky journey to their fishy destination as clearly as the day I drew them, and neither the many, many pictures I have since drawn, nor the hundreds of children's pictures I have since studied, have ever succeeded in rubbing them from my memory.

I must have been about ten years old at the time of the episode of the cats, and almost immediately after it, I left the school to attend the local grammar school. My new school had less than a hundred pupils, mixed, and a staff of five teachers including the headmaster. The pupils were mixed in more ways than in sex. They ranged from eight to eighteen, from fee-paying pupils who could barely read a primer on admittance, to 'scholarship' boys whose brilliance deserved the university career which the headmaster held up before us as the nearest thing to heaven we could ever hope to attain on earth. Towards the celestial cities of Oxford and Cambridge some very few of us actually set our faces, though with far greater hindrances in our paths than ever Christian encountered, and with far less hope and faith to sustain us, for it was pitifully obvious how few ever got there. During the eight years I was at the school, only one of my fellows ever reached the dizzy heights of a degree, leaving Oxford as a B.A. and a Mus.B., only to throw up scholarship to join the R.A.F. and be one of the first pilots killed in the Second World War.

Here, no more than in the primary school, should our failures be allowed to shadow the magnificence of that staff of five devoted teachers. The headmaster himself was a man able and willing to teach anything and everything with equal success. He was an Oxford man, an M.A., an M.Sc., and an A.I.C. In those days before degrees became ten a penny, we felt we could be proud of him. He collected more addenda to his name as his life went on (J.P., etc.), and a story once went the rounds of the school that an impertinent ex-pupil had addressed a letter to him as F.T.A. Esq., A to Z. He was the one man I ever knew who really held science and art to be of equal importance to life. To him education was a process which stopped only when the heart stopped, and the body rested for ever. 'Your true education will start only on the day you leave school,' he would tell us. 'You have simply been coming here to learn how to learn.'

He and the other four taught us everything from Latin to Agricultural Science, from Needlework to Applied Mathematics, and 'drawing', of course, now called 'Art' on the timetable. The laurel leaves had given way to endless permutations of a cube, a cylinder, a pyramid and a sphere, all made of wood and painted white. To the mysteries of 'shading' I was not initiated; it was taken for granted that I knew all about it. At the end of each term an examination revealed my artistic ability to be worth no more than 10 per cent marks.

Then one of the masters died suddenly. His successor, straight from one of the northern universities, was, I feel sure, appalled to find that art was his pidgin no less than the geography he had specially undertaken. We also were appalled, for the accustomed pyramids and spheres now gave way to a deck-chair, drawn in every conceivable position from every conceivable angle.

I shall never know whether Mr. F.T.A., A to Z, could no longer endure the feeble efforts of the new master, or whether that gentleman himself could not and would not attempt the impossible any longer. Whichever it was, there came a Friday afternoon when he and his deck-chair failed to appear, and in their place came the headmaster, literally staggering under a load of original oil paintings. He stood them in a row against the wall, commanded us to take up a position where we could all see them, and demanded our opinions of them. Naturally, we hadn't any. He grew excited as our abysmal ignorance of the visual arts became more and more apparent to him; he even grew angry, though I think this was because he suddenly had realised how he had failed us, rather than any feeling that we were failing him. But the magnitude of the task of introducing us at this stage in our education to the world of art was too much even for him. When the next Friday afternoon came, he came, too, but without any pictures. Instead, we settled down to a double period of applied mathematics, which subject, for the rest of my school life, filled the time allotted to art on the timetable.

We were all a little surprised, at the end of that term, after we had finished our examination in eight subjects for the Oxford School Certificate, to be told that we were to have a school examination in art. Once more I was told to 'bring something to draw *or paint*'. The magic lay in the last two words.

I had no paints worthy of the name, for until that time I had never needed them except for map-making: but my brother had. He had always had the urge to draw, and spent a good deal of his time executing caricatures of our neighbours on the walls of the barn when he should have been dressing corn, and on the newly papered walls of his bedroom by the light of his candle in the early hours of the morning when he should have been asleep. His twenty-first birthday was several years behind him, and a family of neighbours had marked the occasion by giving him a box of good paints. They were a greatly valued treasure, and I knew he would not lend them, but that did not prevent me from borrowing them. Then I stole one of my mother's treasures, too—a perfect, half-open Madame Butterfly rose-bud.

Into the painting of that rose-bud went the same zest that years before had carried the cats towards Yarmouth; but it was intensified now by a conscious urge to create, and a desire to crystallise the folk-culture, of which I had always been vaguely aware, into some positive existence. What I produced was, in fact, no more than a reasonably good pictorial resemblance of a rose, and I doubt if it had any quality about it that I should now characterise as art; be that as it may, when the results were read out the next morning, my name headed the list. Later that morning the headmaster came to my desk with my painting in his hand. He was a little surprised at my sudden progression, as in a country dance, from the very bottom of the set to the very top. I could not then put into words, as I now have done, the reason for my sudden 'success' as an 'artist'.

'It's a funny thing,' he said to me, 'but I have always thought you ought to be able to do art. Why have you not produced this sort of thing before?'

There was only one answer, the same answer which so many, many children could still give to their teachers even in these art-conscious days. At the risk of being considered impertinent, I gave it.

'No one ever asked me to', I said.

II

Let no one imagine that this small success had set my feet on the road to Art. In fact, at this time I had no idea that I ever wanted to get there. For one thing, the results of the School Certificate examination I had just taken turned me from a very mediocre

7

pupil into a promising scholar, apparently, almost overnight. The faithful five had once more scented university material, and were away in full cry before I had really had time to realise that I was the quarry concerned. In my first year in 'the sixth' I had one companion, but the next year I comprised the form all alone. Needless to say, during those two years I never once handled a paint brush, for that would have been a WASTE OF TIME. At the end of the two years came an equally successful Higher School Certificate. The university was in sight, but the two years I had spent in the sixth had been the worst two years of agricultural depression in history.

My father had a small fen farm, containing some of the best land in the district. For the last two years, every potato he had grown had rotted down and had had to be spread back on the land. As I cycled the five miles to school every morning, the very air was tainted and the whole fen stank of rotting potatoes. Every day brought a new disappointment, and often a new financial crisis. A truck of celery, containing five hundred rolls, each consisting of twelve heads of celery such as only the fens can grow, had been sent hopefully to Covent Garden. After ten days or so, the salesman wrote to the effect that he would be obliged if my father would forward the sum of fifteen shillings, as the celery, sold at $\frac{3}{4}d$. a roll, had not quite covered the cost of its carriage to London. During the last two years of my school life, I had been given a bursary of £16 a year by an encouraging County Council. I had been allowed to bank my quarterly allowance intact against the day when I should need fitting out for my entrance to the world of scholarship. But when harvest approached, the need for a new horse on the farm became pressing. There was simply no help for it, and my £32 went a long way towards the cost of a beautiful piebald mare. It was obvious, even to me, that the end had come. There could be no university career for me, and even a training college course was ruled out of question. I had to get a job, become self-supporting immediately.

The headmaster's testimonial to me was full of gentle bitterness. 'I anticipated that she would, on leaving us, proceed to a university, but I now understand that she wishes to obtain a post as an uncertificated teacher', he wrote. He could not have been entirely ignorant of the distress in the fens which surrounded his small island of learning, but pride and self-reliance are two outstanding characteristics of the genuine fen-tiger, and none of my family ever considered the possibility of appealing for help. Years afterwards, when I paid a visit to the head and his wife, he asked me what had been the cause of my sudden change of purpose. When I told them the truth, they were grieved beyond telling, and explained that had they only been told at the time, they would have moved heaven and earth to have made my entrance to the university possible, even had it meant actually borrowing the money in the hope that I would one day have been able to pay it back.

As for me, like the Duchess of Malfi,

> My melancholy seemed to be fortified
> With a strange disdain

and in this mood I set off to teach the junior class in a small village school in Essex, not having had one single minute's training or preparation to uphold me in facing a class of thirty-odd children ranging from seven to nine years old.

Once a week I had all the boys between the ages of seven and eleven inclusive in one room for 'art', while the head teacher had the corresponding girls for needlework. Girls, it seemed, did not require art in their education, but it was something the boys could mess about at, while the girls did the necessary needlework. Little as I knew about teaching anything, I knew less about teaching art. Yet on the very first day on which I faced my new art class, I made a momentous decision. The sight of the familiar green and white drawing books was too much for me, and without even asking permission I removed the lot, tore them up, and handed back to my astonished pupils the separate sheets of paper. Whatever else happened while they were in my charge, the children should not be presented, week after week, with their smudgy, finger-marked and tear-stained failures of the past.

A cupboard yielded a set of small boxes of watercolours, which my predecessor had been afraid to use; and for four years I experimented, knowing that better things than laurel leaves and deck-chairs were possible. I had only a fumbling sort of instinct to guide me, however, and we did not get very far. I could laugh aloud now at the thought of some of the atrocities we perpetrated then, but I am also touched when the head teacher tells me that the art in the school has never been so good since I left.

I was anxious to return to my family, and as soon as a post was advertised nearer home, I applied for and got it. My job was to teach the 'backward' class of the school, and to be responsible for the art with the boys of the junior department.

For me, at least, the headmaster of this large full-range school was a difficult man to work with. He was a strict disciplinarian who had been an officer in the army in the 1914–1918 war, and he ran the school as if it were a military establishment. Wearing three gold watches, all with chains to match (one in each waistcoat pocket and the third on his hip), he stood with a watch in his hand to clock the staff in twice a day. Should anyone fail to be in school fifteen minutes before the bell rang, he was greeted by a figure with a lowering lower lip and a watch in each hand. On one occasion, when a blizzard had held up the return of a master from the north of England after the Christmas holiday, he was greeted by all three watches and a roar of 'Mr P., you are a day, two hours, and forty three minutes late'.

There were rules about everything. No teacher was allowed to speak to another teacher in the corridors of the school, even when partaking of the cup of tea at morning playtime, which was served for those teachers who could escape duty long enough to drink it. It was dispensed just outside the door of the head's study, and if the sound of voices reached him in his sanctum, he would pounce out of it like a bulky black spider, with cold, paralysing eyes. He stalked the corridors on pussy-feet, with a cane concealed under the back of his jacket and the handle curled over his collar, peering through the glass pane in every door, on constant watch for naughty children or dis-obedient staff.

One can readily see that such an atmosphere was not con-ducive to any art, let alone any experiments in creativity. Nor were the actual conditions. The number of boys in the art class was never less than fifty, and at one time reached sixty-four. They had to be jammed as closely as possible into their heavy, iron-framed dual desks, and were bound by the same rigid rules that applied to any class, whatever the subject. Getting out materials and putting them away was done, like drill, to num-bers, and once the class was seated, no one was allowed to move again except the prescribed monitors for the day.

I cannot really remember what I did during those lessons. I was too depressed, too constrained, too irked by senseless rules to care much, anyway. Apart from these formal art lessons, I had charge of 'the sink', that is, the class into which not only those children who were by nature a bit slow, but also those, however intelligent, whose naughtiness disturbed any other class, found their way. Here my instinct served me well, and with a temerity that surprises me now, I encouraged illustrations in note-books concerned with other subjects. With perception

11

rare in him, the head did not interfere, and though he never said so, I really believe he recognised, as I had discovered, the value of 'art' as a part of general education. (The quotes round 'art' are really still necessary; the children I teach today would roll on the floor and shriek with laughter if anyone called the very best of the illustrations that my class then produced 'art'.)

The war broke out, and in the general furore I suddenly found myself married. I returned to work after the summer holidays that year with a different attitude towards it and towards the boss, whose temper had not improved by the prospect of losing all his male staff. I knew I could not endure it for long, and just before Christmas a small incident became the last straw. On the evidence that my register blotting paper bore unmistakable signs of having been used to blot addresses, I was accused of writing my personal letters in school time. (I had, in fact, used one of my precious free periods to send each child in my 'sink' a Christmas card, taking the names and addresses from my register; I had used the nearest piece of blotting paper without thinking.)

I allowed the accusation to stand, and an hour afterwards, when the dinner bell released me, I walked straight to the education offices and handed in my notice.

Soon afterwards the hot war broke out, and with it a string of domestic crises; altogether life became quite difficult. One thing stood out very clearly as a possible solution to the worst of the problems—I had to have a house. Houses were very difficult to come by, because this was the very peak of the evacuation from London and the other industrial cities, but one hope remained. There were still a great many tiny villages up and down England where the school was in charge of an uncertificated teacher, and most of these tiny schools had houses (of a kind) attached. In desperation I began to apply for every such post, where an unqualified head teacher was offered 'living accommodation' as some small recompense for the enormous responsibility she undertook, and a sop to the conscience of the committee which offered her such miserable wages for so important a task as the education of all the children of the village. It was unfortunate for me that a good many town teachers had also thought of the idea at the same time, but Kingston village was really too rural and off the map to attract many suitable candidates. There were four applications for the school there (as I was told afterwards by one of the managers), and the interview I attended on a bright July day, driving behind an aged pony in a dilapidated buggy borrowed from the grocer, would make a story in its own right.

The managers did not, apparently, like the look or the sound of me very much, for they offered the vacancy to each of the other three candidates in turn, but all refused it after inspecting the house. At last it was offered to me, and I would have taken it had the accommodation offered been a dog kennel. It was not a great deal better. The house was falling down, the rusted stoves hung away from the walls. The floors were so bad that it was impossible to stand a chair within a foot of the wall anywhere, and gravy trickled from your plate on to your lap because the table could not be made to stand level. The bus service to the village was non-existent, except on Saturdays, and there was no help in the house because everybody, man, woman and child, worked on the land. There was neither gas nor electricity, and water had to be coaxed from the village pump. The school, in very little better condition than the house, had about thirty on roll, because at that time there was a considerable number of evacuees from the slum dockyard areas of London still in the district, although the great majority of those evacuated at the beginning of the war had found the stillness of Kingston a greater ordeal than German bombs, and had returned to Bethnal Green.

The children ranged in age from four to eleven, and I was the head teacher and all the staff combined. Besides my new responsibility for the entire education of a whole community, I had a six-month-old baby to cope with. Two things upheld me. From some depth inside me there rose to the surface a conviction that I had become what I had always wanted to be, a village school-marm (though I should not have admitted it before), and a feeling that of all types of scholastic career, this was perhaps the most worthwhile in itself and the most rewarding; secondly, though I was as yet completely cut off from it, Cambridge, the celestial city of my youth, was only seven and a half miles away. I don't know what difference it could ever have made to my existence at this time, but I never failed to be comforted that at any rate I now breathed the same air as those who had managed to enter the university.

There was also an infinite relief that though, as yet, I had no idea how I wanted to conduct the school myself, I was my own boss and at least I did not have to follow the antiquated ideas or idiotic regulations of others. On the first day of my life at Kingston, I went eagerly into school to take stock of the materials ready at hand for me to begin my new era of teaching. Half an hour later, I made my first entry in the log book, recording in a neat hand that I had now taken charge of the school, and that a thorough search of the cupboards had revealed the only available equipment to be about a dozen exercise books and a bundle of infant 'sticks'.

III

For the next three years I struggled alone to bring back some kind of life into the school. The teacher before me had been dying of cancer of the spine for the last five years. The school records and the memories of her still left in the village both show her to have been a good, sound, old-fashioned teacher in her days of health. But constant pain and frequent long spells in hospital had told their own tale, and for the last eighteen months the school, already inundated by the waves of evacuees, had been left to a succession of supply teachers, some of whom, according to the log book, stayed only a few days at a time. No one had been responsible for anything, and supplies, difficult enough to get in any case, had been completely neglected. The children had lost interest, and had become bored and lazy: they were too apathetic even to be naughty. There were no less than seven children of eight who could not read a single word, and those of tenderer years, of course, had had no chance to learn anything. Class teaching under such conditions was worse than useless; every child had got to have what amounted to private tuition. I had to keep twenty-nine busy, somehow, while I taught the thirtieth to read.

I requisitioned some white kitchen paper and some thick black pencils. When they came, the pencils, delivered from the education office, were the kind one usually meets only in an election ballot booth. I still wonder if an enterprising clerk in the education office solved a difficult problem by raiding the returning officer's stores during the coffee break. Armed with these, I could tell the children who had nothing else to do to 'draw something' while they waited their turn for my attention.

I did not set the coal scuttle in front of them, but when they asked the inevitable question 'What shall I draw?', I was as stumped for an idea as they were. Neither they nor I had got into the habit of thinking of art as a spontaneous and natural mode of expressing our attitudes to the life going on around us. No child has ever asked me 'What shall I talk about?'; but we all still thought of art in terms of pictorial representation, with an unwritten but accepted law behind us, the result of tradition of drawing in schools, that there were some things suitable as subjects for art, and some not suitable. What usually happened was that day after day they would produce microscopic tanks, armoured cars, ships or aeroplanes of most primitive design, all stranded in a desert of white paper. The pictures themselves were not much more interesting than the laurel leaves, but there was a difference. These were done in freedom, and enjoyed. Gradually the atmosphere of freedom began to have its effect on the children, and now and then a child would put into his picture the driver of his train, or a military policeman holding up a convoy of armoured cars. Finding by experiment that I approved of such boldness, they experimented more and more. I was still so much concerned with the basic skills that this revolution took place around me almost without my knowledge.

Then one day, I was turning out a cupboard drawer which for countless years had been the receptacle of odds and ends that no one knew what else to do with. In it I found a cardboard box full of the remains of what had once been pastel crayons. Not one piece was more than three-quarters of an inch long, and they had rubbed together till they were all, on the surface at any rate, a uniform, dirty grey. Now pastel drawing is an acquired art, and pastel one of the last media I should now choose for children, as pastels tend to be messy in use, produce messy pictures, and cannot be kept without expert spraying with a good fixative. But to the children who had by this time discovered that drawing could be exciting, those bits of pastel were what the cooling stream was to the panting hart. Colour had come into our lives.

At the end of that week, the children and I took a 'nature ramble' round the village. Colour was in the very air, for it was the last week in October, and between the riot of trees and stubble lay sunshine so golden that it was almost pink, charged here and there with transparent smoke, the colour of moonstones, from autumn bonfires, while in the distance the shadows had begun to take on the tint that would soon turn to November blue. I think it was the first time that the children had ever been fully aware of their surroundings. When we returned to school, by common consent we began to put into double harness our new awareness and our enthusiasm for drawing. Without the pastels it would have been impossible. Some children drew round the edges of leaves they had collected and cut them out. Some made cut-out sheaves of corn; I hastily stuck two sheets of paper together and another child drew and coloured poker-like trees, on which to stick the leaves. I suggested to one boy of about ten that the centre-piece of the picture should be a horse drawing a cart full of sheaves. He was aghast that I should ask such an impossible thing as that he should draw a horse. But reading resolution in my face, he got on with it. His tacit obedience paved the way to a flock of migrating birds, a nut-laden squirrel, and even a farmer, who

> Stamped his feet and clapped his hands
> And turned him round to view his lands.

When it was finished, the result (to us) was glorious and beautiful. We had pinned it on the wall, and were standing back in rapt admiration of our own cleverness, when the door opened, and in walked the 'advisory teacher'. She was almost as spellbound as we were.

Her obvious surprise at the work we had produced gave me a good deal to think about. Until that day, I had been unconsciously accepting two premises: one, that art could and should, and undoubtedly would in time, play a much greater part in education than it had done up to the present; and two, that it was the fault, both of my stars and myself, that I knew no more about it than I did, for I was sure that the work I was doing with such poor materials, in an attempt to rouse children who had been so long neglected, must compare very unfavourably with the art in the larger, better equipped and more efficiently staffed schools all around me. But the advisory teacher's gasp of surprised admiration and her few words of guarded praise had suddenly revealed to me that while my first premise was right, my second was wrong. I was not 'all behind', either in ideas or in technique. I knew as much about the technique of art in schools as any of my rural colleagues, to put it modestly, which means that none of us knew anything. But by instinct and sheer luck, I had stumbled into the stream and was already going in the right direction when the wave of 'children's art' overtook me. I had been sent out in the wrong direction, swimming against the tide, and very hard work I had found it. Now I was going the right way, I knew, but I had no one to guide me. That was still to come.

IV

The war was over, and a new age of educational administration about to begin. One morning, a circular letter from the education office contained the news that an art organiser had been appointed to the county's advisory staff. The news roused not even a glimmer of hope or excitement in me. There had been organisers and advisers before, and there still are. The new name meant nothing to me, and even the fact that the new person was attached to the subject I was now so interested in hardly caused me to lift an eyebrow. I have no doubt that to many of my colleagues she may still be 'just another organiser', and the fact still remains that any teacher worth his salt does not want to be 'organised' himself, nor to have the subjects for which he is ultimately responsible 'organised' over his head by someone who only sees the school for an hour or so a term, and who has only a fleeting glimpse of the individual character of the school in question. Nor does any adult human being ever really want to be 'advised' or even to take advice, though he may ask for it. The terminology applied to these worthy people damns their work from the start; but in the eyes of the ordinary teacher they have even greater faults. It is true that most of them have been teachers themselves, but the very nature of their jobs demands that they should have been *specialists*. Their new jobs lift them to a position of some authority, and in doing so usually magnify for them the importance of the subjects to which they, personally, are attached. In turn they visit every school (and in districts such as ours there are almost as many types of school as there are schools), giving advice which is unsought and, what is worse, not understood anyway, tactfully refraining from either praise or candid criticism, but leaving behind them when the door closes the impression that they will expect to see a great improvement in their particular subject by the time of their next visit. Now multiply the effect this treatment has on an overworked jack-of-all-trades like the average village school teacher by the number of organisers, and you will see that the general result is not one that is likely to make the teacher feel more capable of doing his job well. On the contrary, he is usually convinced that because it has been tacitly pointed out to him that there is room for improvement in his teaching of most of the subjects in his curriculum, he must be a noodle and a failure and a misfit and that it would be a great relief to mankind in general if he were to find himself a better-paid job in the local boot-factory. (It takes a strong mind and a magnanimous spirit to interpret the situation correctly, and to see it as an enormous compliment that is being paid to him; it is being implied that he is capable of being a specialist in every subject.)

It was not long before the new art organiser visited my school. She was quite unlike any other organiser I had ever met, both in appearance and manner. Without the smallest particle of humbug or false modesty, she managed to convey to me that she understood perfectly well that without the co-operation of the teachers her job was pointless, and that she was grateful to any who welcomed her help. Then, after asking my permission, she addressed herself direct to the children. Here indeed was a revolution, but it was nothing to what was to follow. She had brought with her a portfolio of children's paintings, which she began to hold up and talk about in turn. The children and I were spellbound.

After a few minutes of looking at this picture of the victory parade by a girl of ten, and that flying fairy by a child of six, I began to be so ashamed of what till that minute I had called 'art' that I had to seek excuses for myself. Worse than that, I began to want to disbelieve that the pictures I was seeing were actually the work of children. I did not say to myself, as I afterwards heard another teacher say, that I expected Miss N.Y. had done most of them herself; for one thing, a sort of peasant honesty in me rose to challenge such unworthy thoughts, reminding me that I ought to expect integrity in another member of my own profession, and asking me rather pointedly if I had never heard the story of the fox and the sour grapes. For another thing, the paintings themselves had the true ring of honesty—inexperienced as I was, I could feel it and respond to it. (The converse is now true; I can detect *dis*honesty in a 'child's' painting at the first glimpse, whether the dishonest element has come from a helpful parent, a teacher overanxious for 'good' results, or from a too precocious effort from the child himself. It is a most useful asset to possess in these days of ubiquitous exhibitions and competitions of children's art, when every village flower show has a children's art section, and judges, at least in rural areas, few and far between.) Thirdly, there was N.Y. herself; a person whose integrity was less in doubt from the first moment, I have yet to meet.

20

In my second attempt to excuse my own ignorance and lack of enterprise, I changed my tactics. I remembered that the lady before me held an A.T.D. That meant years of study at the Slade; it meant that she only taught art; that she had never had to bother with problems in arithmetic, capital letters and quotation marks, famous sailors and the parables, the life stages of the bee, the Amazon basin, the necessity for cleaning one's teeth, button-hole stitch and tonic sol-fa, compensatory movement and morning prayer: nor did she have the extraneous duties of adding up the register, balancing the dinner money, counting the milk bottles, interviewing irate and ambitious parents, smoothing down the cleaner, mopping up Johnny when sick, binding up Mary when wounded, and all the other hundred and one jobs that fall into the one pair of hands of the teacher in a single-teacher school. Moreover, I had visions of an art room specially equipped for that purpose, with sinks and easels and unlimited supplies of paint: and lastly, since I knew that N.Y. had come to us from a grammar school for girls, I imagined what bliss it must be for anyone to deal with a class of selected pupils all one sex, all one age, more or less all of one ability.

These and many more like arguments have since been put to me on all kinds of occasions when I have been the one holding up the pictures. But I have a tremendous advantage over N.Y. because I can always drop the bombshell on my questioner by telling him (much more usually her), that I, too, have until recently been the head teacher of a one-teacher school, and that all the work I am showing has been produced in that school; and that what I am trying to sell them is not just art, but education in its widest sense.

I did not say these things to N.Y., however, on that momen-tous day, though I am sure she heard them hundreds of times before and since. One cry only did I raise.

'Isn't it a great deal easier to produce work like this when you are an artist yourself?' I said.

Miss Y. smiled a cool sort of smile, as if this, too, were an argument for which she was prepared.

'Can't you do it?' she said.

I was trapped, and I knew it. On a similar occasion I had got out of it by saying that nobody had ever asked me to, but I was too old now to blame others for my plodding along the same narrow groove. I replied, hesitantly, that perhaps I could if I tried.

Miss Y., who had probably been expecting a modest denial, threw back her head and laughed aloud. Then in a conspiratorial whisper she added, 'Nearly everybody can, you know'.

To prove this, she organised a course of practical lessons for teachers in the county, beginning the next term. It says a good deal for her initial success as an organiser that no less than sixty of us volunteered to attend ten lessons a term for three terms. Sixty was too many for one class, so we were divided and N.Y. cheerfully undertook two nights a week instead of one. There we were introduced to the delights that should await every child on his entry into school, as well as to those whose acquaintance he ought to make before leaving.

The sixty enthusiasts had reduced themselves to thirty by the beginning of the second term, and in the third term there were only nine stalwarts left; but we were a band of true disciples, who had learned by now that the truth we were seeking was worth the trials we endured. It had certainly not been easy for most of us, and my own experience was typical. To get there I had to park my baby on a neighbour, chase out of school at 4 p.m. prompt, run half a mile to catch a bus, and stagger another half mile at the other end carrying all my equipment. After the lesson was over I had to wait an hour and three-quarters for the only bus returning in our direction. Then I had to walk the last part of the journey, for most of the year in the pitch dark, through tree-shadowed, unlit country lanes, arriving home at about 9.30 p.m.

In spite of all I learned, I can remember very few incidents about the course, though one remains. On the evening on which we were first invited to paint a picture out of our imaginations, 'Autumn' was one of the subjects given. I had that very morning watched my father digging in my garden among the red leaves of a fallen Virginia creeper, and I decided to try to reproduce the scene. In my picture the creature purporting to be my father had one foot firmly on the ground, while the other rested on his spade in the time-honoured way of men digging (in pictures). But try as I would, I could not make his legs 'look right'. In desperation I appealed for help. N.Y. came and looked at my picture (than which any of my seven-year-old pupils could do better), and putting her finger on the leg on the spade, said, 'Which leg is this?'

I too regarded my work of art, of which I was really terribly proud, and after a moment's deep thought I replied, 'It's his front leg.' When the laughter around me had died down, I was given a minute's lucid explanation of the part light plays in the representation of round form. Two or three strokes with my brush had put the legs right, but it was not that that had been valuable. In that minute I had seen a true teacher at work: I saw, crystallised, the attributes of a good teacher, which apply equally to every subject on the timetable. The first requisite is that he should know what he is trying to teach. This is fairly easy for the specialist, but not impossible for the general class teacher. It means that to be worth one's salt in school one has always to be actively engaged in the process of educating oneself until the day one is presented with a wheel-chair by the old pupils as a mark of merit for long and faithful service; it means an open mind on such subjects as space travel, and humility enough to learn from one's pupils, who know far more about it than the average teacher; it means the ability to reason and to judge which parts of one's own mass of accumulated knowledge are suitable for the children in one's present class; it does, in fact, mean that one should be a really 'educated' person in every sense of that overworked word.

The second requirement of a true teacher is the ability to pass on the knowledge one has when and where it is needed, and in as few words as will suffice, unless the class is obviously in the mood for a two-way discussion. How the children of my own generation ever sorted from the bushels of verbal chaff under which they were buried for five solid hours a day the few grains of the wheat of knowledge they managed to assimilate, I cannot understand. Unfortunately, there are still too many people who regard 'to talk' and 'to teach' as synonymous.

Thirdly, a teacher should realise that his function is still to teach. I apologise for making such an obvious statement, but it must be said. We have passed, quite rightly, from the era of being taught to the era of learning for oneself. This is perhaps the very essence of modern education, and the two following sections of this book will, I hope, convince anybody who reads it that I am wholeheartedly in favour of it. But it does not, and cannot, alter the function of the teacher. It has not changed the essential function of the doctor of medicine that instead of standing helplessly at the bedside of a child dying of diphtheria, he now gives the child two inoculations to prevent it from contracting the disease. No one is foolish enough to regret that one very rarely has to fetch out a doctor in the middle of the night to perform tracheotomy by the light of an evil-smelling oil lamp: on the contrary, everyone rejoices that the knowledge and skill of the doctor have been available at the time when they would do most good. Yet there are hundreds of thousands of people who cannot, and will not, admit that the treatment of ignorance has undergone a change as radical as the treatment of diphtheria, and that the practitioner in each case still has a job to do.

Those who regret the wholesale-instruction methods of their own schooldays, no doubt also regret the lack of the bedside manner of the modern physician. They would be better employed if they spent their time thanking God that there is less and less need for either. However, when all is said and done, the day has not yet come when the doctor tells his patient 'I am only here to see that you cure yourself', nor is the teacher in school just to mark the register and to see that the children teach themselves. He is there to see that they *learn*, and the difference, though subtle, is enormous.

To return, once more, to the story of my journey to the world of children's art. At the beginning of the next academic year, it was announced that N.Y. would repeat the course of art lessons for those who could not get in the year before. I applied immediately for permission to join again. N.Y. came to see me, explaining that the places had to be given to those who had not been before.

'But in any case, *you* don't need to come again', she said. '*You know art!*'

We both laughed at this enormous over-statement, and both understood perfectly what was meant by it. I knew enough about it to want to know more, and I had enough technical ability to go on experimenting. I shall never 'know art'. My knowledge of the history of art is still almost non-existent, my visits to galleries few and far between. I have not become an artist myself, and never shall; but without false modesty I can now claim to know children's art. I know more than that: for I know its place in education as a whole, and this is something N.Y. could not have taught me. I learned it

25

from a teacher even greater than she, experience. As Tennyson says,

> All experience is an arch wherethrough
> Gleams that untravelled world, whose margin fades
> For ever and forever as I move

and my lessons are by no means at an end. The following sections of this book are attempts to garner the experience I have gained. I had discovered, when I was ten, that it is a mistake to rest on one's laurels.

⤙ 2 ⤚

The village to which I had come was a tiny community of less than a hundred and fifty people. It lay half a mile from the road leading to Cambridge, and had all the appearance of having been forgotten and left to its own devices while the rest of the world whizzed frantically round it. It was old, but not 'olde'; pretty, without being pretty-pretty; and rural, without being 'rustic'. The lath-and-plaster cottages with their thatch or old tile roofs were homes, not picture-postcard or calendar houses. The school was the ugliest building in the place, and even that was mellowed by a hundred years of wear and tear, and by the ivy which covered a host of architectural and structural defects.

It was made up of one room some thirty feet long and fifteen feet wide, and two tiny porches, one at each end. There was no piano; two old, high, narrow cupboards housed everything the school possessed, and their doors would not close because they were warped out of shape in every dimension. The desks were dual desks, shod with iron, except for one or two in which the real 'infants' sat, and they were of a still earlier period, being the long, narrow type at which six babies could sit in a cramped row.

The windows were all too high to see through without the help of a chair (they still are). I remember the first occasion when an unusual noise from the free world outside attracted my attention, and without thinking I hopped up on to my chair to see what was happening. The expressions of shocked incredulity

27

on the faces of the children at my doing what they had been so strictly forbidden to do for so many years made me laugh aloud. The noise was occasioned by an army convoy passing, a sight which in those days was too common to cause a stir even in Kingston, but the alacrity with which the children accepted my invitation to climb on to their own desks and share my view must have turned several of my predecessors over in their graves. From that moment the children knew that a new era had begun.

Of the 'usual offices' it is better not to think—except to say that the one great legacy left to me at the school was the school cleaner, who, when the school closed after eighteen years, was still with me. I am proud to call her my friend now, and in those early days I relied on her more than she knew. No words of mine could ever do justice to her greatness and nobility of character. Speaking of her one day another friend of mine, who has spent a long life in good works and has claims of her own to sainthood, remarked, 'If, when I die, I find Lucy waiting to welcome me into the next world, I shall know that I have got to a place far better than I deserve.' Because of Lucy's ceaseless and uncomplaining labour, the offices were kept spotless, but as she herself confesses 'it was 'osses work to keep 'em so'.

Most of the children at that time were the children of the village labourers, with a sprinkling of evacuees who kept on leaving and being replaced, so that for the first few years it was difficult to see the overall pattern. After the war, when transport improved and conditions became more reliable, the school settled down to the pattern in which, with minor variations, it remained until the end.

I made note in 1958 of the school as it existed then, and I think that year would be fairly representative of the previous fifteen years, except that the roll stood a little higher than usual just then. There were twenty-six children on the roll, fifteen boys and eleven girls. In age they were as follows:

Five at ten years   Three at seven years
Five at nine years   Five at six years
Three at eight years   Five at five years.

A social cross-section revealed that of these children, six came from 'professional' homes; two had parents who were self-employed, one being the daughter of a hairdresser and the other the son of a market-stall trader. The other eighteen were children of farm workers or general labourers. The significant thing from this social viewpoint was the total absence of any representative of the farmer class. Such children went either to private schools in Cambridge or to expensive boarding schools where their ambitious parents paid high fees for the same education they could have got free on their own doorstep. I would defend to the last ditch, the right of such parents to do what they considered best for their own children at their own expense, but it seemed to me that it did not augur very well for the future health of the rural community that while the notable scientist's daughter and the eminent professor's son rubbed shoulders and held hands with their peers among the children of the labourers, the offspring of the accepted leaders of such a community were being educated, as creatures apart, in a town.

Looking at this batch of children with an eye open for special difficulties, one saw quite a different pattern. Of the twenty-six, four were Italian. Three brothers came from one family, and a little girl from another. All heard nothing but Italian spoken at home, but all were bilingual within twelve months. One of them, however, was E.S.N. (educationally sub-normal) and had a speech impediment into the bargain—not a very easy child to cope with under language difficulty. Another English boy, who was also a special E.S.N. case, was brought to my school by the county child psychologist in the hope that the family atmosphere and the well-known (notorious?) freedom of the school might prove therapeutic. I believe that it might have done so, in time, for he actually attended school every day for about six weeks, a thing unknown to him before. In that time he had dragged a girl up and down the playground with a running noose round her neck, squashed many tiny infants against the rough brick wall with his huge bulk until their noses lost the skin, and deposited the oldest Italian boy on the top of a hot stove while I had slipped out for a moment. That incident proved to be the last straw. My patience and sympathy gave out and I rounded on him, reviewing, as I had to, the havoc he was creating in a school previously running so smoothly. I quarrelled with the welfare officer, demanded an interview with the child-psychologist, only to find that he was leaving the county and was not being immediately replaced, so there was no help from that quarter. At the end of the day, I retired to bed in a state of nervous collapse. I need not have worried. When the boy got home he told his mother what I had said to him, and she rang me up the next morning to say that her boy would not be coming any more to a place where he was not welcome. We were saved—and Angelo hadn't even had his trousers scorched.

Then one must take note of the range of intelligence. At one end was a girl who had the advantage, by heredity and environment, of a 'university' background. At seven she could answer in a flash such questions as 'If 36 is two-thirds of a number, what is the number?' She could do anything except sing in tune, and though she was perfectly aware of her inability in this particular line, she never made any bones about trying, and would sing a solo in the school concert with complete aplomb, secure in the knowledge that she would be judged solely upon her effort to do her best as others were in the subjects which she found so easy. At the other end of the intelligence range was a boy to whom numbers, as such, would never mean any more than Babylonian hieroglyphs to me, though he was quite a good reader. On one occasion, I had spent a long time with him playing games involving the simple fact that twelve pence were the equivalent of one shilling. It was hard work for both of us. At the end of half an hour we packed away the coins we had been using into my purse, and I wrote in his number book the only little bit of abstract number work I asked of him that day

$$12d. = 1s. \ 0d.$$

I explained to him most carefully that this was how we wrote down what we had learned that day, and then left him. Five minutes later, I happened to pass him, and asked him what I had written down. He had no idea, so somewhat sharply I told him to rack his brain to remember what I had said, and that I would be round again in a minute or two to hear the answer. He wept bitterly at my cruelty, but reading resolution in my tone, he applied himself to the task. He suddenly called out that he knew it now. Delighted, I quietened the other children to hear him give the answer. He held up his tear-stained book, blew a very runny nose, and read

Twelve d's are I sod.

I gave up.

It has always been a matter of wonder to me how the older children learned to concentrate in spite of the noise and commotion made by a group of healthy, happy infants at the other end of the room. It was nothing to us that I should be struggling to help one child with an abstract arithmetical problem involving compound long division at my desk, while two feet in front of me a girl wrote a poem 'out of her head', on my right two noisy infants played 'mothers' with much dramatic incident, and on my left a boy of five hammered heartily at two

31

pieces of wood to make an aeroplane. The hammering distracted nobody, but the cries of rage and distress when it was discovered that the aeroplane had been nailed securely to the floor brought us all to the rescue. It was a wearing, tearing life, but if I may be permitted the cliché, there was never a dull moment.

The description of the school as it was during the last few years should throw some light on the difficulties of my first few years there, when all those I have mentioned in 1958 appertained, plus those of evacuated children, no amenities, and supplies at a minimum. I have already described one or two of our early successes in art; the gradual assimilation of the idea of controlled freedom and constructive activity began to put new life into the children, and lessons took on a new freshness. For one whole winter I spent my evenings making apparatus for reading and number, pressing my mother and father into service whenever possible. My father patiently constructed the larger pieces with his gouty old hands, such as a pair of balances out of the stand of my 'companion set', two sandwich cake tins, and a length of lavatory chain, while my mother made doll's house furniture, or cut and stuck, under my direction, paper birds and animals and trees on to pieces of cardboard saved from cereal boxes, to make number dominoes. I was still working on the schemes left by the former head-teacher, awaiting approval of my own new ones from 'the office', and the history prescribed for that part of the term was 'a lake village'. I knew very little about it, and found it uninteresting, with the inevitable result that the class was bored too. I was already bold enough to throw overboard anything I did not enjoy, but common sense told me that in this case it was not the subject so much as the pedestrian approach to it that was at fault. What we wanted was a model, but there were no materials, and even the Israelites could not make bricks without straw. However, it seemed to me that a model was the only way of revivifying this particular bit of dead history, and a model we had to have. The garden was full of clay, after all, and with a little persuasion my patient father dug up about a hundredweight, washed it and strained it, and left it in a heap on the playground to dry out. Next Monday morning it was a mass of hard lumps mixed with crumbly dust, and obviously useless. While we stood shaking our heads over it, a school-manager/small-holder acquaintance came up to the fence and bid us good day. We explained the situation to him. He pushed back his pork-pie hat from his cheery red face and said 'Whoi, now, I reckon as I'm got the very thing. Them soldiers down at the searchlight camp left a gallon or two o' camouflage paint in one o' my ditches. I don't want the blarm stuff—I reckon if we mixed some on it with this 'ere clay, d'y' see, it 'ould stop it from drying and cracking.'

A few minutes later he returned with a gallon can of War Office paint, and my father with a couple of shovels. All the morning the two old men worked. (I could hear them through the open window, grumbling on and off about all these new-fangled ideas in education, but delighted to be in it all the same. 'If there wa' anybody as I 'ated when I were a child', I heard Bill say during the morning 'it wa' my school teacher. I'd as leave a-met the bloody davvle a-coming down the street, as I'd a-met 'er'.)

At the end of the morning we transferred the queer mixture of mud and browny-green slimy paint to a place prepared by me for it—the top of the two infant desks covered in brown paper. Then with jackets off, shirt sleeves rolled up, aprons and anything and everything I could find in my rag-bag tied round them for protection, the children for the first time in their lives experienced the joy of handling a really plastic substance. We created an island and pastel-blued a lake all round it on the brown paper. I explained that we now had to invent ways and means and find materials with which to make causeways, piles, stockades, huts, canoes, etc. Materials came: used match-sticks; strips sliced from mother's kindling; dried Michaelmas daisy stalks, straw, hay, twigs. Soon the lake village was complete, and canoes rode on the paper water. But there was one serious lack—the lake village was still uninhabited. How could we create figures?

That night my mother showed me sadly the result of her day's labours in the house. We had actually got some new stair-carpeting, and it had been put down that day. But our stair-rods, brought from a larger house, were too long. My father had had to fetch a saw and saw the ends off every one. There they lay, forty-eight of them, little shaped ends of wood. 'I may as well use them for kindling', said my mother, sweeping them into her apron. She dropped one and I stooped to pick it up for her. It was in the shape of the head and shoulders of a man. I clawed them out of her lap. Pipe cleaners served for arms and legs, and scraps of material brought by the children dressed them. Anything suitable was stuck on for hair, and our model was finished. Again, the advisory teacher (who afterwards was promoted to the title of the County Inspector, to distinguish her from the lesser organisers who only supervised one subject), making her termly visit, was the only judge of our work. She was genuinely impressed, and even brought round some other teachers to see it. I do not think they were very inspired by it, but that did not matter to us. It was what my children really thought of it that mattered to me, and they thought it was marvellous. Consequently I thought so too.

Our new-found consciousness of the value of art and creative work in general education was leading us farther afield all the time. My first few attempts at making my requisition allow-ance go round had taught me what expensive and frustrating things ordinary exercise books are; poor quality paper, in uni-form, uninteresting covers, with rigid and unvarying ruled lines, though complicated to order in small quantities because different widths of line were used for number and English, and different again for infants and juniors. It was the lines that worried me, and I took the momentous decision to order, in future, plain unruled books for everything, so as to be able to encourage free, unhampered illustration wherever the children thought fit. There seemed to be no point in complicating the issue by having lines for number work, so in future we used plain books for everything. Those of my colleagues who followed my example for English (and they were *very* few—old customs in school die hard) drew the line, literally, when it came to Arithmetic; but I can report with perfect truth that neither the subject nor the neatness which so many teachers think the criterion of good work suffered in the least. Children are the most adaptable of creatures, and the more one asks of them, the more one gets. The plain books were a great improvement, but they still had the same sized pages, and the same old covers. I had by this time begun to find out that there were many more kinds of paper available than those I had previously been accustomed to find in schools, and I had ordered a fair variety with which to experiment. I soon discovered that for English work the ideal was for each child to make his own book, choosing the size, colour and texture of the paper for himself, according to his age and needs. I have since tried many different ways of making the books from the separate sheets of paper, but I have never found a way better than the one we started with, the simple sewn book which every child of six and over can make in a few minutes for himself. We use sugar or one of the cover-papers for the outer cover, which is then decorated or not as its owner wishes. In this way we made our first home-made exercise books, and used them for illustrated journals of our daily happenings, but this was only the germ of things to come.

The awareness of art as a medium for the understanding of other subjects next led us on to a new interest in 'nature study', undreamt of before, and many were the home-made books filled with beautiful, though child-like, representations of wild flowers, birds, insects and pond creatures observed from nature with the aid of a magnifying lens, no longer as 'something to draw' but as things to be appreciated, absorbed, and remembered. These drawings were no more like the laurel leaves of my childhood than is the new-hatched dragonfly to its larva.

Art for its own sake went forward by leaps and bounds under the stimulus of greater experience, freer supplies, and the encouragement of N.Y., from whom I continued to learn all the time. I grew bold enough to tackle subjects in 'art' that previously would have terrified me, knowing that if I really got into difficulty a postcard or a telephone call would bring her to help. Just how much her enthusiasm and encouragement had meant to me I had not fully realised until, at the end of the academic year, she suddenly ceased to be quite so available. This coincided with my shattering discovery that our supply of paint had run out, with a whole term to go before the new supply arrived. Our history for the term had been on the subject of 'The Romans in Britain' and I had just organised the top juniors into a team to paint a long, co-operative frieze of a triumphal Roman procession, when I found that the paint had all gone. I cast about for inspiration. It was spring time and we had been colour-washing some of the rooms in the house with the crude kinds of distemper that were the only kinds available then. The colours were white, cream, buff, and beige. I commandeered all the remains and with them the frieze went on. Togas in a variety of subtle shades were achieved by mixing the distemper with the last remaining dregs of our paint, and blue ink powder mixed with ceiling-white coloured the sky. But the picture lacked the dark tones, and we had no dark pigments left. That problem was eventually solved with two tins of shoe-blacking, one of black and the other dark tan. It was a fairly good picture, but somehow lifeless. I looked down at it while the children crawled about it on the floor, putting in the finishing touches, a brown sandal here, a head of blacking curls there. Suddenly an agitated voice rose above the general din. 'Mrs Marshall,' it said, 'I think the Emperor's wreath has slipped.' I went to look. The information was correct. What had the moment before been just another Roman, indistinguishable from the rest except by his being seated in a chariot, had become the most pompous, triumphant, bacchanalian old rogue of a conqueror imaginable, wearing his crown of laurels at a rakish angle over one eye.

A few days later I had the first of many such letters from N.Y., saying that she was too busy to get out to see us, but needed some examples for a lecture she was giving. I packed her up some of those I thought worthy, including the Roman frieze. I put in a letter in which I said, 'You may find the frieze a bit odd; but my art muse languishes for want of a breath of encouragement, and the children's for want of paint.'

The answer, by return of post, said, 'Your muse must have sat up again when she heard our cries of delight at the Roman procession, and I hope the children's may revive when you get what I am sending you.' She was as good as her word. The education committee had put into her hands a small amount of money to be used at her discretion for art materials where they were needed most. Thereafter, we were never actually reduced (by need) to using distemper and shoe-blacking again. But in any case, I had found out that one can create pictures out of almost anything. The other thing that the frieze had taught me was that there is no limit to the permutations of effect one can get by simply mixing the different colour media at one's disposal. Paint over wax, wax over paint: wax crayon and ink, paint and ink: pastel and wax, chalk and paint, ink and chalk—there is no end to the variations. In passing I should also like to say that there is also no limit to the variety of subjects the children will tackle with complete confidence, providing that their early experience is full and free enough, and likewise no bounds to their skill. Courage and enthusiasm will carry both teacher and class along roads they never dreamed were open to them before.

I was being educated all over again by the children I was supposed to be teaching. Now and then I would stand back and try to see objectively the educational revolution taking place all round me, in which I was caught up as a participator, not merely as an organiser. The school in my charge was now like no other school I had ever seen or indeed heard of. All kinds of things were happening over which, it seemed, I had little control; or, to put it in another way, it appeared to me that if I were to exert any control as I had until then understood the meaning of the word, I should not only nip the buds, but parch the very roots of a wonderful flower I had discovered growing under my feet.

There were matters about which I had a sense of guilt, being, as I had been until then, what is called on testimonials 'a conscientious teacher'. My new schemes of work, for example: they had at last been returned from the education office approved and even commended. But in the interval of time we had found freedom of approach to education, and to attempt now to use set schemes of work based on a rigid four-year cycle with these living children would have been like trying to tie up water in a false-line. The schemes had caused me many hours of thinking, and many more hours of laborious typing with two fingers on an antiquated typewriter; but I consigned them to a drawer in case a school inspector might ask to see them, and forgot them. From that day to this, no one has ever suspected their existence, although I believe one of my near and dear colleagues, a lifelong friend, was severely reprimanded by an over-zealous new 'county inspector' for not having hers constantly brought up to date.

What utter nonsense, what short-sighted idiocy, what criminal waste of time it is for administrators in a central office continually to ask the teacher on the spot for such bureaucratic evidence of his intention to teach! It must be supposed that they justify themselves by saying that they must have some tangible proof that the teacher is doing the job he is paid to do, but it is a negation of all the ideals of education that they should bring it down to this level. The motto of every chief education officer should be another quotation from Confucius:

If you suspect a man, do not employ him; if you employ a man, do not suspect him.

But in any case, a three- or four-year scheme defeats itself by the very nature of what it is intended it shall do. It lays down plans of work for a hypothetical class which it is supposed will exist in three or four years' time. As every teacher knows, no two classes are ever alike, nor the same class alike on two separate occasions, or under two different teachers. Plans can only be made for the class as it is, and only then to cover a period of time easily foreseeable—at the most I would say six weeks at a time. I am always appalled by the contemplation of what the administrators must think of their own usefulness, and the supposed necessity of their being reduced to depending for their existence on such functions as those of approving (or disapproving) schemes of work for teachers who to them are only names, and classes which do not exist yet, in schools the administrators know only as pin-points on a map on their office walls.

The same criticism can be applied to a great many head

teachers, asking their class teachers for the even more ridiculous records of work done in classes. Any head teacher worth his salt should know what *is*, not what has been. If his school has any life in it—and that depends largely on him—he will not need to be told what is happening. It will shout at him from every wall, every flat surface, every desk, every blackboard, and he will be dazzled by the light from the faces of the children. Such H.M.I.s as used to ask for schemes of work or weekly records are fast dying out. The modern H.M.I. sniffs the atmosphere of a school the moment he opens the door, and thereafter follows his nose to his conclusions. Were I an H.M.I., I should regard the existence in a school of carefully filled-in record books as damning evidence of a head teacher who did not know his function, and of teachers obedient but bored, and therefore useless.

Then there was my timetable. It originated in 'the office', and was brought out to me, a large sheet of expensive ivory paper ruled off into dozens of little boxes, all carefully designed to contain such magic indications of possibilities in school as 'Eng. Lit.', or such depressing ones as 'Hymn. Prac.'—each one representing a precious, never-to-be-regained period of time in a child's life. No one has the right to shut the delight of English Literature up in a forty-minute box, anyway, and to know that Hymn Practice has, willy-nilly, to last forty minutes because the timetable says so is enough to make any child consign any and every hymn writer to perdition forthwith. I am not ignorant of large schools, and know perfectly well that in them such a timetable is necessary, because one class cannot expect to follow its own sweet will at the expense of others, and that there are such things as space and equipment which have to be shared: but I suspect that the timetable worship which goes on in a great many of these larger schools is due to the same reason for which many honest and good men follow the religions of their fathers—it prevents them from having to think things out for themselves. When teacher and class are together for any length of time in a room to themselves, the only real timetable needed is the teacher's conscience, and his consciousness of what it is right he should be doing. He is the only one with his finger actually resting on the pulse of his class, and he only can give it what it needs when it will do most good.

I was conscientious about all the wrong things in my early days. I spent hours and hours filling up those little boxes, and casting up sums to fill the spaces below them with calculated information as to how many minutes of the week were to be spent in 'Literature', how many in 'Poetry', how many in 'English', how many in 'Composition'. At last it was finished, and I submitted it for approval to the office. After a considerable lapse of time it was returned to me, signed with the hand of the distinguished education officer of the day, and accompanied by instructions that I was to frame it and hang it in a conspicuous place in the school.

With what was I to frame the precious thing? I tried such relics of the past as I had found decorating the walls on my arrival, but no frame was large enough. In desperation I rolled it up and put it at the back of my cupboard to await more thought and time than I could give it at that moment. A few weeks later a small child brought to me a soggy but colourful representation of bonfire night, but my admiration for this work of art was tempered by perceiving that it had been executed on the back of my timetable. I dried it and put it away, and worried considerably about it; but after a while I forgot the incident. *That was fifteen years ago*, and to date no one has ever asked me for it. There are only two feasible explanations. One of them is that nobody cares a brass farthing about timetables and schemes of work, except to cause head teachers a headache now and again—and that can hardly be true. The second is that in a school where education goes forward all the time in enthusiasm and freedom, it is obvious even to the most casual observer that the school days are simply not long enough to cram in all that the children want to do. In such circumstances it would be insulting to children and teacher alike to ask for proof of how many minutes had been spent that week on table practice or history notes. Those to whom what I have just written seems patent and unnecessary must count themselves as enlightened beings; because for every one of them there are still fifty who worship at the shrine of the fixed and dependable, of the scheme, the record, and the timetable. To such, all I have said will be sheer heresy. If they stick to their stalls long enough, however, they may find that their methods, like an old coat, will come back into fashion. If that is so, it will have been caused by a revulsion against those greater enemies of real modern education, the people who embrace anarchy in the name of freedom, and who find it convenient to believe that no timetable and no record book means, in effect, no work. Let no young teacher reading this get any false ideas from it. To control a class in freedom, to learn with each child instead of instructing a passive class, to be a well of clear water into which the children can dip all the time, instead of a hosepipe dousing them with facts, is the most exhausting way of all of doing a teacher's job.

Until this time I had been so concerned with the school, and my task of 'breeding lilacs out of a dead land', that I had hardly raised my eyes from it to look at the village itself. As the tension inside the school began to ease, I became suddenly aware of an influence from outside the four brick walls of my job. It was as if a pressure were being exerted upon my consciousness by the very hedges and trees, by the bents of grass and the cottage windows, by the church tower and the Jacobean chimneys of the farm. Whenever I walked round the village, stopping at

42

every house, as I did once a week to collect the wartime Red Cross pennies, I felt the presence of something unseen but real. It was just the same awareness of something actually there as I would have any morning when I walked into school at 9 a.m. to find a completely empty, deadly silent classroom; I would know, of course, that every child was there, but that he was holding his breath under a desk or in a cupboard or behind a blackboard, and that I had only to make some remark aloud, as if to myself, about the strangeness of all the children having the measles on the very same day, or something equally nonsensical, to bring them all out, scrambling towards me and crowing with delight, to begin another day of untiring enthusiasm for whatever might happen.

As the village got used to me, and I to it, I recognised the presence. It was the past; not the glorious and epic past, nor the grievous and oppressed past of an agricultural community, such as one might have expected; nor was it the dead-and-gone-forever past, not even the loved and regretted past. The past I felt was a ghost with the spirit and soul of some mischievous child, which hid somewhere along my way, and popped out suddenly to tickle my consciousness and tap on my memory and be gone again before I had time to put a name to it. It crept up slyly and pretended to be the present, and then nipped away again leaving me wondering if there really were any way of telling one from the other.

Mr Eliot has said all this so exactly that there is no need for me to enlarge on it. But when I first felt, as he puts it, that

> Time present and time past
> Are both perhaps contained in time future,
> And time future contained in time past.

I had not read 'The Four Quartets'. When I did come upon it, and found there my own experience summed up for me so precisely, I felt a sense of skin-prickling awe that I should have

43

been enough aware and sensitive to have received the same kind of communication from a place as he did from East Coker, Burnt Norton, and Little Gidding.

I went to the post office and was served by the eighty-seven-year-old postmaster. While he endeavoured shakily to pick up with his skinny, grave-ready claws, the flimsy stamps I had asked for, a grandfather clock in his house struck the hour. Hastily he took out his watch and compared it with the clock. Then he opened the communicating door between the post office and the house and yelled huskily, 'Wife! Wife! The clock's a minute slow.' The postmistress, two years his senior, put out a small, handsome, though wizened face and replied, 'I'm not having him touched. He's stood on the same spot as he does now for two hundred and fifty year, and I reckon you'll be a bit slow as well if you last as long as he has done.' I laughed, as was required of me, but through the open door I could hear the tick of the clock exactly as I might have done had I stood there at the moment when Queen Anne really died.

At the gate of a cottage I would pass the time of day with another ageing lady. When she discovered that I had sympathy for 'old things', she took me inside her cottage and showed me the shawl in which her great-grandmother had been married. 'They were married at the church here in the morning,' she said, 'but after that they didn't know how to spend the rest of the day. So they walked into Cambridge to see a man hung.'

All roads lead to the churchyard, and the church contains this living spirit of the past no wit less than the tiny cottages. It has none of the cold grandeur that so many beautiful churches have. Even empty it defies all feeling of solemnity and pomp, almost as if the Host there were inviting you to come in and warm yourself, and take a look at the new pictures. The pictures are in fact about five hundred years old, and have suffered badly at the hands of the Philistines. But they were painted in a merry hour, and if you look up to the mural above the chancel arch, where in most churches of this period you may see the doom of the wicked, being roasted in hell, you will see instead the most charming company of angels, happily swinging censers, holding up goblets, and best of all, playing musical instruments—harps, and what look for all the world like recorders. Then if, on coming out of church, you decide to call on Mrs W. on the green, you could open the door of her fifteenth-century cottage, and failing to find her, search the house until at last you came upon her in her bedroom, where the painter of the church frescoes left evidence of his very real, flesh-and-blood existence by trying out his brushes and his colour over the six-foot chimney beam. Then, after spending an evening hearing stories of Mrs W.'s childhood in a wealthy Victorian household, and handling rare books of such antiquity that past merged completely with present, one would see with a shock that the clock stood at only a few minutes from another midnight, and hurry away across the village green where a new moon was setting behind a row of Cambridgeshire elms and the chimneys of another farm from which, legend reports, the builders looked out and saw the smoke rising from the great fire of London in 1666.

This, I thought, is what tradition is, the condition of the future being in the past. This is what we inherit, not the benefits or ills of the past, which are but unimportant details, but the power of time gone before to nourish and sustain us in our own time.

I reviewed, in the light of my new awareness, my previous mistaken attempts to teach history, and for the first time I saw, as Lear bids Gloucester, 'feelingly' what the teacher's function with regard to history really is. It is to make each child to realise that history is like a coral reef, composed, it is true, of things that are dead, but in itself still living and growing; and to show him his own life and those of his playmates and peers as the polyps being woven by time into the topmost patterns. Once a child has understood that 'history is now and always' the details of the story of the past are his for the taking, or perhaps more aptly, his for the reading. Never again would I deliver a 'history lesson' on this man or that battle. My job was to create a taste for history and to place before the children such an array of tempting fare that they would reach out and help themselves. The lake village and the Roman procession had been steps in the right direction, but steps in the dark. In my new conviction I saw clearly where I wanted to go, and strode out with confidence.

The first and most obvious thing was a history of our village. This had been done recently in thousands of schools up and down the country, and I had seen a few of the results. None had had what I wanted. I was not in the least interested in the 'Queen Elizabeth slept here' or 'Admiral Nelson passed this way' viewpoint, because this attitude localised too much both the place and the time. What I wanted was to meet and make friends with the spirit of the continuous past that accompanied us everywhere we went in Kingston. There were very few actual records to rely on, for Kingston had never been a large and important place, in spite of local stories to the contrary. The whole success of my enterprise depended upon using Kingston as it stands today as a skeleton upon which to hang the clothes of the past, the garment of history, by accepting without fear of contradiction the premise that Kingston in the days of the Roman occupation was the same as any other village anywhere near it at the same time in history: that Kingston during the Black Death might just as easily have been wiped out altogether as its nearest neighbour, which was one of the nine 'lost' villages of Cambridgeshire, and that Mayday games were exactly the same on our village green as they were anywhere else.

So we started a book called 'The Book of Kingston'. It began in pre-Roman days. We looked at the topography of the area, and relating the known Roman settlements and roads in villages nearby, we decided where the most likely place would have been for them to have built in our village. We explored how the Romans lived, and what effect their coming might have had on the village. This was the pattern for the study of the succeeding ages. Whenever a relevant, proved historical detail could be incorporated, I used it. In this way we were able to use touching human tales of people who had really lived in the places all around us. The Danes burning down Cambridge in A.D. 870 was interesting, but it remained the sort of historical fact one could get out of any good history text-book; the lovely, human story of Thurkill the Dane, in the ninth-century version of 'Murder will Out' at Elsworth (taken from Wise and Noble's *Ramsey Abbey*) made the protagonists live again. In the same way medieval Kingston began to appear, not just as a small place mentioned occasionally in official records, but as a place where people actually lived, stories of whom were preserved in the lists of deodands. Of William Walys, for instance, 'who was picking his peas [pears?] in Dane's Furlong, when the ladder broke, and caused him to fall. Price of the ladder, *2d.*' Of Robert Day, of Kingston, who was killed in a quarrel at Sturbitch (Stourbridge) Fair, and buried at dead of night in the pigsty of the prior of Barnwell, and whose murderer, after taking sanctuary in Chesterton Church, later abjured the realm; of the little boy at Toft, our 'next door' village, who was 'carrying two sparrows on a plate', when Elijah's dog jumped up at him, causing him to stumble against a wall. The wall collapsed upon him and killed him. There was much to-do to determine the cause of his death, for upon the decision rested the amount of prayers said for the poor child's soul. Was it the sparrows, which had flown away, or the wall, or the dog? The meeting decided that it was the dog, valued at a halfpenny, but when they went to collect the dog, Elijah had killed it, so the poor little boy went without prayers at all. Medieval Kingston was a joy to think about, mainly because of the church and its associations, and likewise we passed to the fifteenth- and sixteenth-century cottages, the eighteenth-century barns, the nineteenth-century memories of our grandparents, and twentieth-century Kingston as we knew it.

Now it goes without saying that all this took a long time, and that art played the biggest part of all in recording all that we found out and talked about. We reconstructed in our book the church murals as we thought they might have been before Dowsing got at them. Who was Dowsing? Why did he want to cover up *our* pictures? Could we find bits of all the statues that were smashed if we dug in the churchyard? Or discover the stained glass windows that were taken out and hidden, according to village rumour (every village without stained glass has this rumour, of course). What were the seven acts of mercy por- trayed between the spokes of the Wheel of Mercy on the west wall? Who was St George? And St Christopher?

We painted a frieze of the Robert Day incident, and another of Thurkill the Dane. Question and answer, speculation and research went on all the time. Which way did Robert Day's murderer take to 'ye porte of Bristowe', when he left Chester- ton church 'clad only in his shirt, and with a cross of wood in his hand', as 'a felon of his lord, the King'? How far did the monks of the Synod of Ely walk in procession to the field of Lolworth, where Thurkill, swearing falsely upon his beautiful beard that his wife was innocent of the murder of her English son, 'drew back his hand, and with it came off the whole of his beard, drawn out by the roots from his face'?

A new spirit of independence came over the children, and with it self-reliance and discipline. I would miss a child and say

'Where's Jean?' 'Gone to the church to copy a fresco' someone would answer, and I would have no qualms for the safety either of Jean or of the irreplaceable treasures of the church. Painting out of doors became a glorious summer-time occupation. We used to bundle all our equipment into a wheelbarrow and set off to record some cottage or barn pictorially, leaving a bold note for any school inspector who paid a formal visit and found both class and teacher absent. On the cracked old American cloth covering of my desk I would write large in white chalk:

GONE PAINTING. FIND US IN THE FIELD
BEHIND THE CONGREGATIONAL CHAPEL.

The only person who ever accepted my invitation was the divisional art inspector, and one need hardly record his reactions; but in spite of his obvious delight, he let his job get on top of him, I felt. Standing knee-deep in ox-eye daisies and yellow bedstraw, in the shade of elms as old as the chapel or the dove-cote we were painting, he there and then offered me the job of art teacher in a brand new school for six hundred secondary modern pupils just going up in another East Anglian county, using as a bait a lovely modern flat which went with the job. He seemed genuinely surprised by my refusal to exchange the gold for the glitter.

The next year's history started all over again from the same place, but from a different viewpoint. We simply did the history concerned with the village green. Folk-moots, compurgation, forest laws and heriot, crime and punishment (for example, witchcraft and the stocks), fairs, feasts, markets and holidays, and the sad days remembered by the children's grandparents, when food was so scarce that a benevolent farmer sent a load of turnips and mangel-wurzels every day to be tipped up on the green, so that as it grew dusk the mothers of Kingston could creep out and fill their aprons with something to cook for their children the next day. Village officers and their jobs caused much interest, particularly as so many of their occupations are to this day commemorated by surnames common hereabout: Woodward, Hayward, Wayman, Pinner, Pinfold, Constable, etc. Ale-tasters, bread-and-butter weighers, and chimney-searchers were all sketched, from sheer imagination, performing their peculiar duties.

The third year's history was inspired by Hone's *Every Day Book*. We simply called our history 'A Country Calendar', and went through the year finding customs appropriate to villages such as Kingston, according to the months in which they had taken place. The year began with the apprentices' holiday pranks on Twelfth Night, continued with 'Plough Witching' customs on Plough Monday (I could speak from experience here, because I had often taken part in the fun on Plough Monday as a child in my fenland home, and had verbatim reports of the 'straw bear' ceremony when my maternal grandfather played the chief part; by that time the ceremony had become irretrievably mixed with the mummer's play and the version I got was a jumbled mixture

> Here come I, old Beelzebub.
> Pains within and pains without,
> If the devil's in, I'll fetch him out.

So, through the rituals of Shrove Tuesday and Ash Wednesday, and so on, to Mayday. This presented us with such a wealth of exciting detail that May had been left behind long before we had finished with it. Hone gives a marvellous account of an eyewitness description of a Mayday procession in medieval England. I quote in full to prove what a genuine source of real, living history such an odd scrap of reading may provide (libraries are full of such books as will make the real teacher cast aside the commonplace history text-books for ever, though these still have their place in every school as 'private readers' for the children, who can then fit the jigsaw of historical knowledge together and have the very best of both worlds).

'Of the manner wherein a May game was anciently set forth.'

In front of the pavilion, a large square was staked out, and fenced with ropes to prevent the crowd from pressing upon the performers, and so interrupting the diversion; there were also two bars at the bottom of the enclosure, through which the actors might pass and repass, as occasion required:

Six young men first entered the square, clothed in jerkins of leather, with axes upon their shoulders like woodmen, and their heads bound with large garlands of ivy-leaves, intertwined with sprigs of hawthorn. Then followed *six young maidens* of the village, dressed in blue kirtles, with garlands of primroses on their heads, leading a fine sleek cow decorated with ribbons of various colours, interspersed with flowers; and the horns of the animal were tipped with gold. These were succeeded by *six foresters*, equipped in green tunics, with hoods and hosen of the same colour; each of them carried a bugle horn attached to a baldrick of silk, which he sounded as he passed the barrier. After them came Peter Lanaret, the baron's chief falconer, who personified *Robin Hood*, he was attired in a bright grass-green tunic, fringed with gold; his hood and his hosen were parti-coloured, blue and white; he had a garland of rosebuds on his head, a bow bent in his hand, a sheaf of arrows at his girdle, and a bugle-horn depending from a baldrick of light blue tarantine, embroidered with silver; he also had a sword and a dagger, the hilts of both being richly embossed with gold. Fabian, a page, as *Little John*, walked on his right hand, and Cecil Cellerman, as *Will Stukely*, at his left. These, with ten others of the jolly outlaw's attendants who followed, were habited in green garments, bearing their bows bent in their hands, and their arrows in their girdles. Then came *two maidens* in orange coloured kirtles and white courtpies, strewing flowers, followed immediately by *Maid Marian* elegantly habited in a watchet coloured tunic reaching to the ground; over which she wore a white linen rochet with loosed sleeves fringed with silver, and very neatly plaited; her girdle was of silver baudekin, fastened with a double bow on the left side; her long flaxen hair was divided into many ringlets, and flowed upon her shoulders; the top part of her head was covered with a net-work cawl of gold, upon which was placed a garland of silver ornamented with blue violets. She was supported by *two bridesmaidens* in sky coloured rochets girt with crimson girdles wearing garlands upon their heads of blue and white violets. After them came *four other females* in green courtpies, and garlands of violets and cowslips. Then Samson the Smith, as *Friar Tuck*, carrying a huge quarter-staff on his shoulder; and Morris the moletaker, who represented *Much the Miller's Son*, having a long pole with an inflated bladder attached to one end. And after them, *the Maypole*, drawn by eight fine oxen, decorated with scarfs, ribbons and flowers of divers colours; the tips of their horns were embellished with gold. The rear was closed by *the hobby horse* and *the dragon*.

The writer goes on to describe the setting up of the Maypole, the exhibition dances performed around it by the foresters and the milkmaids, the frolics of the hobby horse and the dragon, and the merry jesting of Much and Friar Tuck with 'the lower orders of the populace'. After the procession had withdrawn again, the same 'lower orders' surged round the Maypole in their own right, and 'amused themselves by dancing round the Maypole in promiscuous companies, according to the antient custom'.

My first thought was that here was something that we simply must reproduce dramatically and show to 'the lower orders' on our own village green: but a further glance at the text dashed this hope. No less than thirty-four characters are actually mentioned, apart from oxen and their attendants, and the school roll stood at twenty-four including the newest arrivals, not yet five years old. But we could paint it, in every accurate detail. The frieze which resulted was two feet wide and thirty feet long; every detail was discussed as we proceeded, and I could fill a whole book with the general education which was given incidentally as well as accidentally by this piece of work alone. One small detail must suffice as an example. A girl of ten had finished the character on which she had been engaged, and was looking in the text for the next one to tackle. She read aloud,

'After them came four other females in green courtpies—Mrs Marshall, what are courtpies?'

I had to confess that I didn't know. Together we went through book after book on costume, but without success, though with a good deal of help from the rest of the class, who could never resist the chase once the quarry was roused. At last I said, 'I will ring the County Librarian, and see if she can help us'. For some reason the thought of this intrigued the children a great deal, and there was a dead, most unnatural silence as I explained our need to the County Librarian. (The telephone is in the classroom, as a head teacher's room is a luxury undreamt of in such schools as ours.) The Librarian promised to ring back, and we spent a tense five minutes until the startling bell stopped us in mid-sentence. The result was negative, but not hopeless: the County Library could not supply the information, but suggested that we should try the City Library, and gave us the number. With excitement mounting behind me I got through to the City Library, and once more explained. Twenty minutes passed, hopes flagging. Then the bell rang again. I was a little surprised at hearing a cultivated male voice say, 'This is the University Library. The City Library has asked us to help to solve your problem. Actually, the spelling varies and the garment is usually spelled "courtepy"—a short sleeveless jacket worn over other dress.'

Somebody remarked, 'I shouldn't have thought of using a telephone for anything like that' and the girl whose pidgin the courtepy really was added, 'Or a library. I thought they were places you got books out of to read at home.'

I am not sanguine enough to believe that these children, all by now between sixteen and eighteen, remember what a courtepy is, or even the incident; but I hope that they remember that there are other uses for a telephone than to summon a doctor in urgent need, and that libraries are mines of information as well as never-ending sources of detective fiction. But of course the real value of the incident was the lesson that where there is a will, there is a way, and that interest is the best of all spurs to the will.

I have dealt at length with art and history as an educational duet, simply because the past was so vividly present to me and seemed to be encouraging me to continue along the line I was already upon. It should go without saying that the other subjects were being treated in the same manner, and with the same results. The essential thing was to grasp every idea that would make learning more *active*, and therefore more interesting and more easily assimilated. We had recently had staying with us a student from the School of Oriental and African Studies, who had been sent out to do a month's survey of a rural community in the English countryside before setting off to become an education officer in Nigeria. After he left, he continued to write long letters describing his new life in the Delta Province, and because of this direct contact, we all felt a special interest in Nigeria. Enthusiasm for geography ran high, that term. The children kept on asking to be allowed to paint pictures of life in Nigeria, but in spite of their skill, these pictures were never really satisfactory. I felt this quite strongly, and tried to find out why it was that we were never satisfied with the results, although great interest went into the making of the pictures. It occurred to me that the trouble lay in the scale of the work: because of our personal contact with someone actually living in Nigeria, we wanted to identify ourselves with real life there, too; in fact, we wanted things big enough to get into, so to speak. (If this had happened at a later stage in the development of my experiment, I should have shelved everything else while we went out and built 'Nigerian' huts on the village green, pounding mealies for our own lunch, dressed in dyed curtains and hung about with beads; but at this time I still had not quite broken the collar of my serfdom to the timetable.) As it was, I did the thing that occurred to me then, and very bold it was, considering all things. I suggested that we covered the end wall of the schoolroom with an enormous picture of a Nigerian village, painting direct on the whitwashed bricks. In this way we were able to depict trees large enough to stand under, huts large enough to enter, and life-sized black children playing only a few feet from us, it seemed. Looking south, we saw a framed rectangle of English sky, for the window remained too high to see through to the very end; but looking north, we entered the sunshine and colour of Nigeria. It was as simple as that.

On another occasion, a chance remark was made one day about somebody's uncle from Wisbech. The child spoke as if Wisbech were farther off and of much greater mystery than Lagos. It was quite plain that the older children who had been drawn into the conversation had no better idea, either. I asked how far Wisbech was away from us. 'About a thousand miles', said the youngster whose uncle lived there.

Shocked, I began to ask other questions of a similar nature. I found that though the accumulated geographical facts the children were possessed of were many, wide, and disparate, not one of them had any idea about the size, shape or general characteristics of our own county. We looked at maps, and placed Cambridgeshire in England. We looked at the small map of the county in our specially produced atlas, but it did not make much impression. We took the atlas outside into the playground and orientated it, crowding round to see that the villages we did know were actually in the right direction. It was so small that it defeated us. There we were, standing in a playground which was a narrow north–south oblong, looking at the map of a county which including the Isle of Ely was also roughly a north–south oblong. In five minutes we were organised, armed with playground chalk, and away on a map, sketched on the asphalt in chalk and afterwards painted in with white paint. Rivers were put in in blue, roads in red, railways in black: towns were yellow, villages orange. We studied bus and train timetables, and consulted ordnance survey maps for mileages. The infants brought their own toy trains and cars and had wonderful games crawling up and down the map with them. Perhaps the funniest twist of all was the new look given to the age-old playground game which for some unknown reason has become 'Squashed Tomato' in the language of today. Sitting at my desk one morning I heard the game being played outside. A voice was giving orders to the players. 'John, three scissors south towards Cambridge. Carol, two pigeon steps towards Newmarket', etc., etc. We were all most disappointed to return to school after the summer holiday to find the playground resurfaced and our delightful map gone.

Then there was Greystone Island. I had been struggling to impart some knowledge of contour lines, without much success, although we were by now quite familiar with O.S. maps. The trouble was that we lived in such a flat county that it was really very difficult to relate the lines on the map to the actual countryside. Somehow I had to demonstrate the meaning of all the curious squiggles on our maps. We had a hundredweight of potter's clay in an old bin outside, clay which had been used again and again and had got tired. We used it to create an island. We pinned white paper carefully to a table and then emptied the clay-bin bit by bit on to the paper, moulding the wet, sticky clay into hills and valleys and cliffs and beaches and promontories and harbours and peaks and estuaries (and learning all these geographical terms as we went along). When we had finished, we coloured the paper all round blue, to represent the sea. Then with a mighty concerted effort, we heaved the whole island up just far enough for someone to pull out the paper from beneath it. (I ought to have said that I had intended to do this, and had used very tough paper on purpose, and also that the clay had been allowed to dry considerably before attempting to pick the island up entire.) The paper showed very clearly the outline of the island at sea level: for the first time many children understood an outline map properly. We then made a wire cutter, exactly like a grocer's cheese cutter, from a piece of wire and two pieces of kindling, and proceeded to cut off layers of our clay island. Each time, as we cut it, we placed the lump we had cut off on to the original outline map and drew round it. When we had finished we had a complete contour map of our island which everyone understood. We then used our contour map to construct sections, in the time-honoured way, and when we had completed our graph, from north to south, for instance, we took our wire cutter and sliced the island in half in a north-to-south direction, and saw that our drawn section was a true one. Only when we were satisfied that we truly understood the meanings of contour lines did we allow the clay to harden. Then we played other games with it. We created storms by raining on the island with a watering can with a rose on the end of the spout. We watched where the water ran between the hills, and marked out the course of the rivers. The island had been made of grey clay in the first place, and had been named Greystone Island on our maps. Now rivers and peaks began to be claimed by the chil-dren, and when at last one of the more romantically minded boys invented a cove full of buried treasure, geography gave way at last to English and story writing in particular. Greystone Island's clay became too dry, cracked and crumbled and finally disappeared back into the bin from which it came. By that time, no doubt, somebody had led us away to something new, though I cannot now remember what it was.

I shall be dealing with art and religious knowledge together in the next chapter, because that belongs to the real hey-day of our joy with paint and paper, and at the moment I am still concerned with showing the slow movement of our tentative trials at finding the symphony of the arts a means to education.

The revived interest in learning was making its influence felt throughout the rest of the curriculum. A couple of successes in the eleven-plus examination had tended to make the parents sit up and take notice, and spurred the children themselves to greater efforts. New life was particularly evident in the English work. Gone were the days when groans greeted the announcement that I wanted a 'composition', and when the results read like a mixture of a Victorian 'object lesson' and a foreigner's first attempt to construct a sentence about the tail of his dog. Pens and pencils began to scurry across the line-less pages with more speed and greater enthusiasm if with fewer full stops and less careful 'double writing'. Now and then a startling innovation surprised us all. One day an eight-year-old girl, unasked, produced a poem. I had heard of schools where 'poetry' was written, had had some of the poems shown to me, and did not think much of them.

> I like playing football
> It is a lovely game.
> I play it in the winter,
> And in summer just the same.

As an exercise of more interest and more joy than a composition on 'A Game I Like', I appreciated this kind of effort, but my criterion of poetry was that it should capture something that could not be caught in plain prose, and this kind of doggerel did not satisfy my criterion. I asked myself, therefore, what purpose was served by asking children for it instead of good prose. When I read the following from one of my own children, I knew that what had happened was that feeling had been too strong for ordinary composition, and that the child herself had felt the need for poetry.

> On the hill beside the bank
> There is a little brook,
> But nobody knows but me.
> But nobody knows but me.
> They will never know,
> They never will know,
> Nobody knows but me.
>
> Spring is so sweet and so pleasant as well,
> I can go in a field,
> And smell something lovely.
> And such a lovely smell,
> Such a lovely smell,
> Such a lovely smell,
> All round the field.
>
> Violets and violets, let me look and
>   touch and smell them,
> Love, lovely, lovely.
> And such a lovely smell,
> Such a lovely smell,
> Such a lovely smell,
> Right round the field.

Again, I shall want to deal with poetry and its use in the school in a later chapter, as the true flowering of that art also came with experience; but here was the beginning—by having had the chance to give full freedom to her reactions to her environment, this child had increased the measure of her own sensitivity and was aware that there were art forms suited to whatever feelings she had need to record. Paint and paper were of no use to her to recapture the breath of spring, but words were; and her new percipience told her that poetry was nearer to the scent of violets than what she knew as 'composition'.

It was the children themselves, not I, who discovered how interchangeable the forms of art are. On another occasion I set

59

'My Family' as a subject to be painted, having previously had great fun with the children looking at a Victorian album of family photographs brought to school by one of the children. We had played at arranging family groups while other children pretended to be photographers with cameras hastily rigged from chairs and dusters, etc. The resulting pictures were good as painting, because by this time our art was beginning to be worthy of the name, and even more informative. I had one small boy of seven and a half, who was new to the district and the school. I had had him only a few weeks, and had discovered that he was extremely retarded, though I had good reason to believe that I knew why. His eyes were crossed more than I had ever before seen, to such an extent that one pupil was almost out of sight all the time, and the other by no means straight. I could not believe but that his vision must have been very badly affected, and put his backwardness down to this, hoping to per-suade the M.O.H. that here was a case for urgent attention. It was, however, very plain that Roger's backwardness was not merely in school work, for he could not tie up his own shoe, put on his own coat, or even 'be excused' without help. I also discovered that though he could not recognise a single letter or word, he understood pictures, and knew number symbols, so that he was soon doing simple sums and playing number games with interest, providing someone stayed with him. Moreover, he delighted in pictures, and having dropped into a pictorial world in school, was soon painting away and turning out very good, ambitious pictures for a seven-year-old. After several weeks I had to admit that my theory of his backwardness being due completely to poor vision was not correct. The parents were elusive and as the family lived in the next village in a lonely farm, information did not come easily.

When I picked up Roger's picture of his family, it was a revelation. In the middle of his full-sized sheet of sugar paper was an enormous female figure surrounded by several others of smaller size. In the top right-hand corner was a tiny trousered creature, and another, Roger himself, was placed fairly and squarely within the abdomen of the giantess in the middle. I sat down and talked to Roger about his picture. The tiny man was Dad, who played very little part in the boy's life, because the females other than the mother looming so possessively large were his attempt at representing no less than nine sisters all older than he. His diffidence was in large part due to the constant overmothering of ten loving women, who had never allowed him to do one single thing for himself. He simply had no idea how to *try*, and shied off in terror from anything he thought he would not be able to do.

The parents were persuaded to allow an operation which turned him into a handsome little boy, and after a few bitter days of being made to do everything for himself or go without, he took on a new lease of life. He never learned to recognise a letter, though I enlisted the help of our child psychologist, and efforts to teach him in every known way went on until he left the secondary modern school at fifteen. But in every other way he became a perfectly normal, intelligent and sensitive child. Just before he was to be transferred to the secondary school, he grew quite sad lest his inability to read should tell against him in the new school, and wandered wistfully about with me asking if he really had to go, and so on. Then one day he said shyly, 'Will you let me do something that I like once more before I leave?'

'Of course, if I can', I replied.

'Will you let me do a really big paper mosaic all by myself?'

'Yes, of course, if that's all you want.'

'Can I do anything I like on it?'

'Yes.'

'Will you promise not to look at it till it's finished?'

'Well,' I said, 'I would promise, but I can't see where you could do it so that I shouldn't be seeing it all the time.'

'I could go behind the piano', he said.

Obligingly I pulled the piano away from the wall, and with several sheets of paper, a pile of glossy magazines, and a pot of home-made flour and water paste, Roger retired behind it. The work went on at all odd times, wet playtimes, art lessons and so on for the best part of a month. If in my travels round the class I approached too near the scene of operations, Roger would stick out an alarmed face and say 'Go away. Oh, please don't come yet', and I would hastily retire. The other children kept his secret, though they hinted darkly that they didn't think I should like what he was doing—and I thought I detected a slightly shocked air in some of them. Then one day he came out shyly and said 'You can look now' and held up the picture of the Crucifixion. I can hardly ever remember being more moved. The artist—I use the word literally here—who had produced this magnificent work, worthy, as I have always thought, to be hung in a church alongside our medieval treasures, had been, four years before, little better than an uneducatable idiot. Yet here was deep thought, true sensitivity, sincere feeling and that element of self projection which turns clever technical skill into art. It was as though he had issued a challenge to the world of education to dub him E.S.N. at its own peril, for though it was sad that he never learned to read, the world could better spare many a more literate smart-aleck than this illiterate creative artist. Education is more than the ability to read and write, which is after all only secondary to the ability to think and to feel.

The other thing that arose from the family pictures was also a surprise to me. After playing about for a few minutes with a piece of chalk, one girl suddenly said 'I could write about my family better than I could paint it', and getting up from the floor went to her desk and produced this.

My Family

In my family there are Mummy, and Uncle Bert, Tony, and Janet, Carol, Gay and Jill. There are seven altogether and they work very hard. Mummy does not like washing day, or doing the bedrooms out. The best thing she likes doing is going out for a treat, or something like that. Uncle Bert works on the road doing the grass. He has put earth all over a part of the village green. Tony is working all over the place, and comes home at the most ridiculous hours and Mummy asks him where he's been. He either says he's been to Langley or Wilburton. Janet is working at the post office in Cambridge. She has passed her exam, and is now a telephonist. She works with a lot of boys and goes to work at 8 p.m. and comes home at 6 p.m. and sometimes 7 p.m., and last night she came home at a quarter to nine. Carol will not help Mummy and will not get the rabbit's food, and again I have to get it. She is always kicking me in bed in the morning, and her ears are always dirty. Mummy says she is the best of the family, but I do not think so. Carol says she will never move, not if she can help it, because she has got so many friends here. These are some of them Mrs. Evrettt, Mrs. Schneider, Mrs. Marshall, as well as Mrs. Bell and Prue. When John was here I had music lessons because I am very fond of music, and I still tinkle about a bit on it now. Last night I watched a old Elizabethan play about people being put in the stocks. Now Jill gets her own way too much last week she had 3d. and when we asked for 3d. Mummy said No you mustn't, so now you can just imagine what my family's like.

I came afterwards to accept this interchange between the different forms of art as a matter of course, as something, indeed, to be expected if the children were responding as one hoped they would; but the sudden change from one to another was a new idea to me when Gay let herself go on the subject of her family. Carol's dirty ears and the jealousy of the preferential treatment given to Jill could not be said in paint. Skill in one art was as essential as skill in another. Once that idea took hold, it grew and flourished, and it was not long before 'New English' had arrived, as well as 'New Art'. The children were used to handling paint. Now the same confidence was beginning to show in their handling of words. It was not at all the same kind of English that one can get from children simply by teaching them to play clever tricks with words, substituting long ones for simple ones, peppering each poor little noun with unnecessary adjectives, and making the page look like a hedgehog's back with spiky exclamation marks. It was simply the sheer realisation of what words are for, and what they can do. More and more children made for themselves the same discovery as Prue had previously made, that some things require a form more specialised and more intense than everyday prose, and that that is what poetry is. A closer study of poetry and deeper appreciation of true poetry led to more and more attempts at using it when it was the right form for the thing to be said. It was at this time that Jill wrote her 'Swan'; and it was now that Matthew, aged seven, passed his poetic comment on life as he knew it. His poem was called 'What Goes On'. There was then a sub-title, 'Outdoors, on Water':

> Ducks bob up and down,
> And boats pass by with people chattering.

Then a further sub-title, 'Indoors, On Land':

> Telephones ring and mothers rush,
> Babies cry, children scream,
> Only fathers work.

In prose the most notable thing was the sudden freedom from the conventional 'composition' style and the perfect nonchalance in passing comment that delighted and sometimes amazed me, as I saw things which I had previously taken so much for granted, afresh, through the eyes of the children.

(a) In the evening the sun begins to set and it looks as if someone has been careless and spilt red and yellow paint in the sky. (JILL, 8.)

64

(*b*) A wet hedge smells just like bread and cheese.   (DAVID, 9.)

(*c*) (*Written from the point of view of my Siamese cat, a regular visitor to the school.*) When I was young my owner took me to a place with a funny smell, (Rather ghastly, you know). Well, there I had something which humans call an operation, so that I could not have kittens. I think it is horrible of humans. They don't have their children stopped from being born. I have forgiven my owner because I have found out why it has to be—the kittens would have had to be drowned. But I still don't understand. Children are not drowned.   (SARAH, 8½.)

(*d*) Our doctor is a very tall man and when you are ill he is the kind of man that cheers you up by the way he looks at you. He tries to keep you cheerful. His eyes twinkle each time he steps into your house. For his living he goes round putting people better.   (ANGELO, 10.)

'Honour thy physician for the good thou hast of him, for the Lord hath created him.' Could any doctor want a better testimonial?

Interest in subjects other than those I have already mentioned flared up. I had introduced the children to clay and their paint-experienced hands soon gave proof that they had an instinctive feeling for sculpture. Our first sawdust firing in our own playground was yet another landmark. Then another new organiser had been added to the list of those already in existence, this time for music. Until now we had had no chance of making music except by singing lustily unaccompanied and I fear, very much out of tune. One day the music organiser arrived in a van, with a piano for our use. Hastily we made room for it in the corner farthest away from the fire, a 'Tortoise' stove which was always either stone cold or else white-hot—usually the latter. It took a good deal of pushing and trundling to get the heavy piano into its place over the knotty old floor of the schoolroom. The music adviser leaned breathless on one side of the instrument while I stood rapt on the other side. He caught my eye and said, 'Well, now are you satisfied?'

My answer surprised me almost as much as it did him. I heard myself say, 'No, not exactly. Go back and fetch me twelve violins.'

It would be untrue to say that he did; but I hold it to his everlasting credit that he did not ignore or treat as mad my written request for a set of violindas, which followed his visit. I had seen the Hullah Brown method in action, and I thought it a good example of the way a primary school could fulfil its real function in the scheme of education, which is to create interest, spur curiosity, and open doors through which the children may choose to go in the later stages of their growth. I had no illusions and knew that I should not be able to produce a string orchestra, because for one thing I knew nothing whatsoever about string-playing myself, and the instruments were of the cheapest kind ever produced. But they made a noise when plucked, delighted the children who had never held an instrument before, required that they should be able to read music, however simple, and opened their eyes and ears to music made on stringed instruments on the B.B.C. Our adviser was quite aware that I was no musician, but he did me the honour of trusting me with an expensive experiment. That year we took part in the first-ever string festival held for primary schools in Cambridge. The violinda method afterwards died a natural death and I had to stop using ours for sheer lack of replacements of strings, etc. But the years when we did use them served an invaluable purpose, for they aroused an interest in music which never since flagged. Listening to real music became not only a lesson but a pleasure, and I used my own record player and records for many a 'listening time' with no thought of 'playing down' to the children.

I listened to a Paganini concerto yesterday. I was very impressed by Paganini's music. It was being played by Leonid Kogan, who in my opinion is a very great violinist.

When I heard it, I was immediately drawn, dreaming, into a world of my own. I felt as if I could go on listening spell-bound to this marvellous music for ever. Fancy paid me a visit, telling me that the music sounded like a hunting cat after a mouse. The first music that I heard sounded slow, as if the cat could not find the mouse. In the third movement, the cat had found the mouse and was chasing it, and every now and then the whole orchestra would boom and crash.

(BEVERLY, 10.)

I wanted some recorders, too, but I was told that I could have nothing more. Nothing deterred, we decided to raise some money and buy our own. I had been trying out some puppetry with the children and made up my mind that a puppet-show at Christmas would be the thing to raise the money we needed. Once the idea was accepted, the whole school, including me, caught puppet-fever. I split the school into three camps. The babies, six children ranging from $4\frac{1}{2}$ to 6 years, made potato puppets and put on an impromptu school scene, each puppet in turn singing, reciting, dancing, being caned by the potato-headed puppet teacher, etc., and ending with a slap-stick con-certed version of 'We wish you a Merry Christmas' which itself nearly brought the house down. The 'middle group' of only four children made glove puppets and performed the story of the three Wise Men of Gotham and the imaginary sheep crossing the bridge. The oldest children wrote and per-formed a puppet pantomime based on the folk-tale 'Tom-Tit-Tot'. All the characters were made to measure, so to speak, for the children who had to manipulate them. We had come by a wonderful puppet horse made by a friend of mine at one of N.Y.s classes, and we decided it was too good to be left out. I also had an English yokel character which I had made myself, and I had the idea of getting our difficult boy of the period, whom I shall call John, to use these in the marionette show as well as his own puppet in the glove section. He turned out to be a puppeteer *par excellence*. All was set and rehearsals had begun when a new pupil arrived—the son of a university professor from Toronto, with a very pronounced Canadian accent. He had to be included somehow in the show. Hastily we began to construct a new character, a cowboy, so as not to waste the unusual accent, and before long he was complete, but there were only a few days left in which to fit him into the pantomime, and that without upsetting the parts already well practised and reaching a high standard. The boys themselves solved the problem, as they usually will if given enough encouragement. While Nicky was learning to manipulate his puppet. John fetched out the horse and the yokel. Side by side the sons of the university professor and the semi-illiterate farm-labourer started an impromptu scene. The cowboy strode on, swaggering. 'Jest lemme show you how to ride that hoss', drawled the slow, cultivated, nasal Canadian voice.

'Wass 'e say?' said a perfectly natural East Anglian one.

'I said I know jest how to ride that hoss. I learned out west with Buffalo Bill.'

'I doan't understand 'im. 'E can't talk English.'

With that the yokel climbed off the horse, and the Yank climbed on. Then John came into his own. He played that horse as only a genius puppeteer could; it bucked, and reared and backed and kicked, while the poor cowboy puppet flopped sideways and backwards and got upside down underneath the horse's belly, or wrong way round facing the tail, and was finally flung headlong over the nag's head to the ground, Nicky having long since lost all control of him. Then as he lay on the floor, John, with consummate skill, danced the horse all round him and over him, finally pushing the nose of the horse underneath one of his strings that had got caught up in the air somehow, and heaving him bodily out into the wings.

All this was, of course, impromptu practice; but the sight of

John doing something he really liked doing, his insight, his quick perception and his speedy reactions, his wonderful sense of fun, was a revelation to me, and something of a miracle. When I regained my strength lost from sheer exhaustion of laughter, I congratulated both the boys, and told them that I wanted it practised hereafter exactly like that. I think it never reached the peak of perfection of that day again, but suffice it to say that 'on the night' when we reached this point in the show, it was stopped for several minutes by applause, and one grandfather had to be taken outside to recover his lost breath.

I cannot let this mention of our puppets pass without recording our greatest triumph, which was a marionette Nativity play. Several years had passed since we had done our first puppet pantomime (which had supplied the recorders we wanted), and we were becoming old hands at puppetry by the time I attempted such an ambitious project. We told the story of the Nativity simply with the aid of our puppets and carols that we already knew, making our characters, apart from the obvious ones, fit the carols rather than the other way about. The children least clever with their hands each made a shepherd, and the crude, unkempt reality of their creations added a touch of marvellous sincerity to the shepherd scene. This was the highlight of the piece. The angel Gabriel had been made entirely by an eight-year-old girl and had been dressed by her in white silk with opalescent sequins sewn here and there to catch the light. I suggested that he should be given large wings of silver metal foil, and a halo to match was suspended on his head strings so that it hung above and behind his head, but did not touch. The result was a distinct success, and Gabriel's slow descent from the dark-blue star-spangled sky to the crouching unsuspecting shepherds below was a great moment.

I had asked a local electrician to come and fix some lighting for us, and in spite of being himself extra busy with Christmas displays in large shops in Cambridge, he gave us his precious time on his day off. When I offered to pay him he was quite hurt, and said that if he couldn't do a little thing like that for children it was a pity. Then he went off home, to come back later in the day with a perfect little electric star, so constructed that we could move it across the back cloth in the scene in which the Magi met in the desert to follow their belief to Bethlehem. With the electrician's clever help, we were able to have a fire, round which the shepherds stood. When Gabriel made his entrance from above, we were able to take out the rest of the lighting, leaving only the glow of the electric-bulb-under-red-cellophane of the shepherd's fire. Effective as this was, the children were somehow not quite satisfied. At the last rehearsal but one, someone said wistfully, 'Wouldn't it be lovely if Gabriel's wings really did shine in the dark?'

What? Well, *of course they could.* As soon as school was over I hared into Cambridge and bought some white luminous paint. Hastily we painted thickly the back of Gabriel's wings and halo, and the hem of his robe. Then we left him under an electric light bulb to absorb all the light he could until we needed him.

The angel host had been made by the simple device of having dozens of smaller crêpe-paper and silver figures all on one large control, so that one movement of the puppeteer's wrist lifted every wing on one side at the same instant.

On the first of the three consecutive nights on which we performed the show, the audience consisted of people invited specially—those who I knew would for one reason or another be particularly interested in this from an educational point of view, and those who simply qualified for an invitation by being special friends of the school. Amongst them was a man who qualified under most of the headings equally—an artist, a teacher, a religious man, and a personal friend.

The moment came for Gabriel's descent. The glow of the fire died down, and the immobile puppet-shepherds loomed heavily towards it. Behind them Gabriel lowered in the darkness, nothing but a pair of slowly moving wings and a wavering, suspended halo of phosphorescent light. Goose pimples rose on my own arms, and the gasp from the audience told me of their reaction. The next moment all the lights were back, and to the singing of 'Ding-dong, merrily on high', the angel host appeared. When the show was over, the gentleman previously mentioned sought me out straight away. Holding both my hands in his he said 'I would not have missed it. That angel scene—.' He paused, struggling to hold back emotion. Then, 'Straight from the heart', he said, 'Straight from the heart', and made hastily for the door and the covering darkness of the school playground outside.

The next night parents and friends of the children packed the room. The third night was open to anyone who wished to come, and we proposed on that night to take a collection for a local charity. By the time we were ready to raise the curtains of our home-made puppet proscenium, the school was jammed with people as I have never seen it before or since. All the audience of both the previous nights had returned, bringing with them their friends and relations. How they all squeezed themselves in I still cannot imagine, and I have often wondered how many more shared the same fate as the husband of one of my friends. His wife had been on the first night, and at her instigation he had come the eight miles to see the show after a long day's work. He was a little late in arriving, and in spite of being a large and healthy physical specimen, he was absolutely unable to force the door far enough open to make his presence known, because of the press inside. So after struggling vainly for ten minutes or so to open the door, he had to confess himself beaten and return home disappointed.

71

I cannot let the account of this puppet effort go without just one more tale, this time from the teacher's personal point of view. No one who has ever undertaken to do a puppet-show of any kind, however small, will need telling what an amount of work went into an effort as ambitious as this one. A month before the appointed time, all the marionettes were complete and in their first glory, but a solid month of daily practice reduced them one by one to broken playthings. The children themselves worked like Trojans to put right the accidents that every day brought forth to our little actors, but there always came the time when dusk was falling and they had to be sent home and I was left alone to mend broken strings, put on new head controls, and so on, ready for the next day. The worst time of all was during the last week or two of the making stage, when all the slower children had to be helped because practice couldn't proceed without them, and all the finished puppets, being used by hands as yet unskilled, were broken almost every time they were taken out of their little calico bags. Time was already beginning to press, and I found myself sitting up night after night into the early hours making and remending puppets when all the rest of the day's school and household chores were finished. I was getting desperately tired, but on a Sunday in November our new rector was taking a service in the church at evensong at 3.30 p.m., and I felt an obligation as well as a desire to go. I arrived a little late, and as my usual pew had been filled with another family, I went up to the front of the church, almost under the pulpit, where there was an empty one. The quiet and peace of the church began to work on me, as it always did, as soon as I entered. I got down on to my knees for the general confession, resting my forehead on the pew in front of me—and woke up in the middle of the sermon. My sheer exhaustion was due to too much anxious puppetry, but only when the show itself proved such a success did I admit, even to myself, that I had perhaps as much excuse for my lapse as Eutychus had, though it was one of the many virtues of our new parson that he did not make his sermons overlong.

I am sorry that if by remembering and thereby recelebrating some of our successes I have given a false impression that we went from strength to strength without a large proportion of failures, but it would surely be stupid to commemorate them, so I can only state baldly that they existed, were very real, and sometimes seemed difficulties of such size that they appeared in prospect to be insurmountable.

There were the parents who at first did not trust the new sort of education I had introduced, and who clung in a sort of resentment to the kind of schooldays they themselves had had as being the ideal. There were the usual difficulties attendant upon my being 'a foreigner' to the village; and people who had no children and were therefore not directly involved with me in any way took it upon themselves to try to check the rush of change which had overtaken an institution that for so long previously had remained static. Such tiny pin-pricks as the incidents were in themselves festered into deep wounds in my mind when things were going wrong and I could offer at the moment no tangible proof that what I was doing was in any way an advance on what had gone before. Then I would doubt my ability and in the middle of a sleepless night resolve to return forthwith to formal, common or garden instructional method, and to leave pioneering to those more fitted for it, and less involved with the too-close adult world of a tiny rural community. Of course, my resolves were quite worthless. I could not have stopped, if I had ever tried; but it is true that I never did try, for at 9 a.m. the next morning the tide of children and a new wave of enthusiasm would sweep me off my feet and I would be swimming ahead before I knew it.

Just as a small and quite unimportant example of one of these incidents, I will tell the story of the picture frames. When I inherited the school, there were on the walls two large, framed, glazed photographs of their late majesties King George V and Queen Mary. When N.Y. came, she decided that better use could be made both of the frames and the wall space in every school, and bought a lot of lithographs to brighten up the dingy classrooms, at their worst after years of inevitable neglect because of the war. In this way we came by a rather amusing lithograph by James Fitton, and a prosy, dull one of some gliders on Dunstable Downs, by whom I cannot remember. These were duly inserted between their majesties and the glass. As time went on, we became just as used to these pictures, and as bored with them, as we had been with the royal faces, and forgot that they were there. Then one day when N.Y. arrived unexpectedly, she took a delighted look round at the fresh, gay work of the children decorating wall space everywhere, and inquired what on earth 'those ugly pictures' were doing amongst it. Weakly I protested that the frames were too high and too heavy for me to lift down. I remember the look of withering scorn on N.Y.s face as she piled desks and chairs on to each other to reach them down herself. The glass of one was broken in the process, and into the cupboard they went to await repair. That year, after the parish meeting had been held in the schoolroom, I had a visit from the parish chairman. A question had been raised at the meeting as to the whereabouts of the beautiful pictures of the king and queen which ought to be on the school walls. The meeting had deputed the chairman to ask what I had done with them, and the inference was that they were part of the village tradition over which I had no control. The feeling roused by my refusal to re-instate them surprised me, used as I was to village life and interference.

There was trouble over italic writing, which many parents had never seen or heard of before: some objected to my way of teaching subtraction, and others thought me disgusting because I allowed, and even encouraged, their children to take off their dresses, shoes and socks on scorching summer days. But mostly the cause of their antagonism was, I felt, a deep-seated mistrust of me because it was obvious that the children were fond of coming to school, and of me personally. It was made only too evident to me that the adult population of the village did not believe that any good work could come out of a school where the pupils were not mortally afraid of their teacher, and that if the children were enjoying doing something, then 'work' was not the right word to apply to that activity, whatever it was.

The puppet-shows gained me a little ground, I think, and time perhaps did the rest. Whatever the cause, the opposition lessened little by little. Every puppeteer becomes, like Autolycus, 'a snapper-up of unconsidered trifles', and my first intimation that what I was doing was a little less obnoxious to the parents came with bundles of the most incongruous mixtures of oddments—stay-busks, boot-buttons, collar-stiffeners, old bible covers, lace-bobbins, Victorian braiding, lead weights, old stockings, and so on, which arrived from home 'for the puppets'. Nothing was ever refused, and after ten years or so, I had arrived, and open criticism faded away, though I have far too much experience, both as a teacher and as a villager, not to know how lively it was and is among the women at work in the fields, and indeed wherever two or three are met together. In any village the teacher is always fair game for a grouse or two, and if she is wise she takes no notice of it at all, though it takes a strong mind not to retort sometimes that good manners and intelligent behaviour begin, like charity, at home.

I have not mentioned other crafts that we took in our stride, simply because time and space do not permit; but it should go without saying that clay-modelling, paper-sculpture, needle-work, etc., all had their place in our creative world, and that those I did not know about were tried out with enthusiasm and joy, I learning as I went along, with the children, by a process of trial and error.

At the end of the second stage of my work here, perhaps the greatest result of all was in the new teacher–child relationship. I had learned to respect the intelligence, integrity, creativity, and capacity for deep thought and hard work latent somewhere in every child: they had learned that I differed from them only in years and experience, and that as I, an ordinary human being, loved and respected them, I expected payment in kind. Conversation and discussion became one of our chief delights, and above all, we learned to laugh together. And as Rupert Brooke said,

Laughter is the very garland on the head of friendship.

⊷ 3 ⊶

A few years after I had begun to feel myself confident in the matter of teaching children by means of art, I paid a social visit to the small school in Essex in which I had first made my bungling attempts to teach anything at all by any method. The same head teacher was still in charge there, and 'my' job was being done by a young man, who had also undertaken all the art in the school. It was plain to see that the head was not particularly fond of her only male assistant, nor of his brash way of telling her 'how things were done now'. Wearing a rather wicked little smile, she suggested that I might like to spend the afternoon in my old classroom, where the young man would be taking an art lesson. I agreed, hoping to learn something new, and she led me to him, simply telling him that I had been overcome by a desire to spend a nostalgic day in one of the scenes of my youth, but nothing more.

He had already prepared his lesson before I arrived. There were twenty-four dual desks in the room, with two boys in each, ranging in age from seven to eleven. In front of each boy was an oblong of white kitchen paper, about 11 by 10 inches, and on each desk two tall and unsteady paste-jars, one containing a watery mixture of crimson tempera and the other the same pale mixture of emerald green. A jar of water and two small, soft squirrel-hair brushes completed the equipment. When the boys were settled, the teacher told them that they had 'red and green today', and that they were to paint whatever those colours suggested to them.

Half an hour later we collected the results. There were forty-eight line drawings, without one single attempt at 'filling in', let alone any thought of drawing or painting in mass. There were stiff-legged green plants in red pots: green cypher-cats on red cushions: red pillar boxes on green pavements; red cars on green roads, etc. A very few had made some attempt at texture by putting wavy lines in the sea, or spiky veins in the leaves, and these were selected by the master from the soggy pile for my special attention. One particular one he brought to me to be admired. It portrayed a red ship, very rigid and symmetrical, on a pond-like green sea.

'Rather good for a nine-year-old, don't you think?' he said. Now the awful thing was that he really meant it—and who was I to shake his confidence? I was only there for an hour, and could give him nothing to replace any faith he had in himself as an art teacher in that time, if I robbed him of his complacency by confessing now that I knew something about the matter. I decided quickly to assume an intelligent but old-fashioned kind of ignorance in an attempt to draw him into some real appraisal of the work he held. I suggested that I would perhaps have felt happier if the ship had not been crimson. He in turn explained that that was exactly what 'modern art' was, that there should now be no need to paint things pictorially true to colour, and that therefore a red ship was perfectly permissible.

'In that case', I said, rather tentatively, 'wouldn't it be a good idea to have a whole range of colour for the child to choose from? I understand that the same ship may appear to be of quite different shades to two different people, but how can anyone paint the ship the colour it appears to him if he hasn't got the pigment with which to do it?' 'After all,' I added, 'these boys live within reach of the Thames and if any boys know what ships look like, these ought.'

The master's frown told me that he regarded me as an old-fashioned old busybody who was not prepared to accept new ideas, and who, in any case had no notion what she was talking about. 'How could you possibly mix a whole range of colours for each child?' he said. 'It would take all day to prepare a lesson and clear up after it.'

My indignation at his self-righteousness robbed me of some of my determination to be kind. I had to rap his knuckles just once.

'But with the materials you gave him, he could have had three colours', I said meekly. He looked blank, so I went on. 'If you mix red and green, you get a sort of brown.'

Understanding dawned on his face accompanied by a look of horrified amazement. 'But that would have *ruined* the paint', he declared, and turned from me, obviously having made up his mind to give away no more trade secrets to someone as stupid as I was.

I felt mean, then, at having so deceived him, and I feel mean now when I think of all the times I have used that incident since then as an example of all the wrong ways of going to work to produce something worthy of the name of art. (He left very shortly afterwards to take a much 'better' job in Germany, where I have no doubt he is still pursuing his own red and green lines of paint.) But there it was, he had gone wrong in what I consider to be all the three real essentials of a good art lesson: and if art is going to be used as the foundation of a successful, thorough, liberal education in the primary school, then it stands to simple reason that it must be good art.

Where was the poor young man so wrong? As I said before, in all the three essentials of a good art lesson: (*a*) materials, (*b*) presentation of the subject, (*c*) his appraisal of the results.

Let us deal with them in that order.

It may be an aphorism accepted the world over that bad work-men blame their tools, but it should be equally accepted that with good tools good work can be even better. If the tools are right for the job, they lend themselves naturally to correct use, and technique is improved straight away. To know what tool to choose and how to use it is the task well begun, and as the old proverb says, 'Well begun is half done'.

Art is of necessity an individual activity, and materials for it must be as varied as they are carefully chosen. In the lesson I have just described, forty-eight boys were involved: forty-eight *boys*, not the same number of identical human machines guaranteed by science to give off so many identical ideas per second, or to react in identical fashion to a set of given factors set up as external stimuli. Those boys varied in age, aptitude and ability, in background, character, and sensitivity. Yet they were all limited to exactly the same materials with which to work. Now if you had a secret passion for landscape gardening, and all you were ever given was a window-box and a packet of nas-turtium seeds, it would not be very surprising if no one ever discovered that you were a budding Capability Brown. If, on the other hand, you had a gift for writing terse, pithy minutes of the parish meeting, you might be appalled at being asked to write a modern sequel to *David Copperfield*. I have nothing against window-boxes or the works of Dickens, and let me say straight away that I think a feeling for one kind of art is most often the open door to all kinds of experiment with other types of artistic expression; but confidence is the greatest asset a child can have, and confidence in any task can often be gained by having the materials that 'feel right'.

Take the question of the paper, for example. Kitchen paper is good, useful, and cheap, but it is not the only paper on the market. To slit a large sheet of white kitchen paper into four may be easy and economical for the teacher, but is the little oblong that results always the right size and the right shape for the subject to be painted, and even more important, for *the way* John wants to paint it?

If you must always use kitchen paper, at least vary the shape and the size. Then watch the texture of the paper, too, because kitchen paper comes in different varieties from different suppliers. It can be thick or thin, rough or shiny, absorbent or non-absorbent, tough or flimsy. I am no mathematician and could not possibly work out the permutations of variety one could get from shape, size and texture of kitchen paper alone, but the number must be great. However, I cannot see why so many schools should be limited to kitchen paper. I know, of course, that it is the cheapest, but if the cheapest materials only produce poor results, then they are the dearest in the long run.

There are many other beautiful art papers on the market, many of them well within the means of a well-planned budget. They give a range of colour, texture, thickness, shape and size which can in itself be enough stimulus to turn a lackadaisical, couldn't-care-less type of class into a keen and enthusiastic one.

Here is a list of the kinds of paper I have found useful and exciting.

(a) Sugar paper

This runs kitchen paper a close second for cheapness, and therefore is fairly well known. Note, however, that sugar paper can also vary. There are two thicknesses in general use, the thinner one being much the cheaper and not nearly so nice, but it is quite suitable for infants. There is a wide range of colour, though I usually find three shades enough, and prefer grey, blue, and either buff or sage green.

(b) The cover papers (I like Oxford Cover best)

These sheets are larger than sugar paper, smoother and tougher. They will stand up to a good deal of wetting and handling. This paper comes in a wide range of lovely shades, all of them useful, especially for mounting. The quality is so good that it can be used twice, once on each side, as a mount, before actually being used to paint on, so that quite often the same sheet of paper is put to four separate uses.

(c) Pastel paper

Again, larger than sugar paper, delightful to paint on, tough, all shades and black.

(d) Black mounting paper

Approximately the same size as pastel paper, a great favourite with the children and very useful for mounting.

(e) Kitchen paper

As described above.

(f) Frieze paper

This comes in rolls of 20 inches by 36 feet, smooth surfaced, a good variety of shades.

I like to keep a stock of all these kinds of paper, and either choose myself if I am setting the subject and consider one type to be the ideal for the job, or allow the children free choice if I think the subject is open to wide interpretation. In the interests of economy I ask all the children to tell me before starting what type they propose to use, and I only allow the under sevens to use the better papers on special occasions, or when their work has proved them worthy of special treatment for once. In spite of the utmost care, there will be times when the good paper runs out, and even times when all the normal supplies have gone. There is no need to forgo the art lesson when that happens, nor is there any need to spoil all the term's lessons by being niggardly with the available supply in case the paper runs out. When this happens, it is the time to put one's ingenuity to the test, and find substitutes that cost nothing. Newsprint will add an exciting new texture to a picture, providing the paint is used correctly: and the backs of school circulars, old letters, type-script, etc., etc., have all been pressed into service with amazing results. A business executive heard that I was always glad of paper of any kind and turned out an enormous carton of clean-backed cyclostyles that had been in excess of the firm's adver-tising needs, a shopkeeper saved all his large sheets of thick wrapping paper for me, and on one never-to-be-forgotten occasion one of the managers turned up with a supply of arti-ficial manure sacks, the insides of which were lined with a soft, absorbent, thick-fibred paper which was the last word in painting luxury, especially as the sacking on the other side made the works of art very durable, and gave a tapestry-like effect to the whole. Variety is the spice of life, and necessity the mother of invention. All this goes with the question of paint and other media as well as with paper. Use it while it lasts, and when it has gone, use your brains and whatever materials fortune and the children bring you.

The easiest and cheapest way of varying the paper is in its shape. I want to emphasise this particularly because the experi-ence of much lecturing has shown me that teachers are con-cerned more with the lack of composition in the work of their children than with any other aspect. They complain that what-ever the size of the paper they allow their pupils to use, the children still persist in placing very small objects or figures right in the middle of the paper and leaving large areas either com-pletely bare or else filled in with a strong plain colour in which the subject of the picture is overwhelmed and lost.

In the next section I have dealt at length with the subject of an art lesson, and the great care that is needed in presenting the subject to the children. I hope that this advice will go a long way to solving the difficulties of the planning of the picture, but it cannot be denied that some children seem afraid of the outer edges of the paper in front of them.

Even for the boldest of children, the oblong sheet of paper as it comes from the suppliers does not seem to be a very happy shape; in fact, I think I would condemn it as the least desirable for children's work. They always want to begin with the chief object of the picture, which they usually place squarely in the middle, at least until they become the experienced little artists that some of my pupils were at the age of ten or eleven. This attack on the middle of the paper leaves the corners of an oblong sheet too far away, and in some ways quite unrelated to the central figure. A square is a much more comfortable shape, with its entire area much more easily under immediate control. I do not know if it is possible to buy sugar or kitchen paper in square sheets, but it is very easy to cut the oblong sheets into squares, and let me hasten to say that the pieces cut from the ends of the rectangles need not be wasted. These long narrow strips can be used for valuable exercises in pattern making with brushes, felt pens or wide lettering pens, for reinforcing the joins or the edges of mounted pictures, for small objects on co-operative pictures, for individual note-book covers, and so on.

If a child shows signs of being afraid to include the corners, even of a square, the answer may be to cut him a circle. The circle has always been a magic shape to man, and there is no shape more satisfying and calming. In the context of painting, it approximates most nearly to what the human eye takes in naturally. Normal vision does not lie within the arbitrary lines of a rectangular figure. The more experienced my children grew, the more they returned, from sheer preference, to the circle; they learned how to draw a circle for themselves with the aid of a drawing pin and a piece of twine, and would often compose a picture within the circle and then proceed to decorate the corners of their sheet of paper, outside the circle, with patterns. This technique produced a wonderful medieval feeling in the work which was most appropriate when we were doing the *Canterbury Tales* (p. 173).

The very young child's awareness of and reaction to the shape of his paper will be to a large extent unconscious; but as he develops, he can be made more aware of the difference in shapes and sizes, and the suitability of a certain shape for the subject in hand, by a little careful planning on the part of his teacher. A sheet of sugar-paper slit in half longwise produces two long, narrow rectangles. If children are given pieces of paper this shape, and told to use them vertically, they can then be asked to *fill* the sheet with such upright, long subjects as a thin witch, a clown, a man up a ladder, a tall poplar tree, and so on: they will be quick to see how well this shape of paper accommodates this sort of subject. They can then have another identical sheet of paper and use it horizontally, and find subjects to fit this equally well, for example a cat crouching ready to spring, a dog lying asleep with head on forepaws, a boy swimming, etc.

I have always found that given freedom and plenty of practice, children have a natural instinct for good composition. Gay's picture of St Hugh of Lincoln and his pet swan (plate 16) is a good example. She had started on a sheet of sugar paper by drawing herself a margin all round, to as to leave her mosaic framed when it was done. As she proceeded, the lines of the hills and the lake, etc., all seemed to be emphasising the horizontal limitations of the paper. St Hugh's upright figure was not enough to balance the effect, and even the curved lines of the swan did not break it. Experimenting with lines to make the picture feel comfortable, she swept a great halo round the saint's head which went outside the prescribed margin she had set herself. The horizontal line of the margin having been broken by the sweeping curve, she saw how the picture immediately 'came', and although it destroyed her first idea, she left the halo outside the border, with distinct artistic success.

Co-operative work on a large scale, in which the individual objects are executed separately on the children's desks, cut out, moved about on the background sheet until they fit comfortably together to make a composite picture, and only then stuck down irrevocably, is as useful for practice in composing a picture as it is instructive in perspective. One does not set out to teach primary school children one or the other, but if they learn by observation and trial and error that things look better in one place than another, or that the large house in the front and the small one at the back looks right, but that vice versa it looks wrong and uncomfortable, they will go on applying what they learn in other pictures. I am often asked, when displaying some of the very large pieces of co-operative work the children did, how much 'help' or 'instruction' I gave. The answer is, quite truthfully, 'very little'. I gave advice, when it was needed, because I was the only person present who had an overall, undistorted view of the whole work as it proceeded, and did not care whose tiger got in front of whose tree, for instance. If and when I could see that one child's selfish desire to put his particular bit of work right in the front was going to spoil the sensible reading of the whole work, I would stop them and invite them all to stand back and comment on the picture as it stood. They would soon discover what was wrong, and the offender would generally see reason and move his creation further over. When at last the cut-outs were stuck down and the filling in of the background began, the older, more experienced children took charge, and they would often consult me as a member of the team about the advisability of this colour or that placing of a tree, and in my capacity as the oldest and most experienced person there, I gave whatever advice I could. I was always more than pleased if they could do without me altogether.

On one occasion, the older children, helped by a group of the seven-to-nine age range, had set themselves out on a large, 8 feet square panel depicting a fox-hunt in full cry. The horses and riders, hounds and fox were all drawn and painted on the individual children's desks. The twelve large sheets of paper had been stuck together on the floor to provide the background for the picture, and the blackboard T-square used with accuracy to arrange a 6 inch border all round and so provide a frame, as we had learned from experience how difficult it was to mount such large creations. The exciting moment for the horses, etc., to be put down and arranged had come. I was out in the playground with the babies, engaged in reading a story, but keeping tags on the industry inside the school by interpreting the noise coming out of the open window. Suddenly I heard a loud outcry of dismay and chagrin, and hurried in to see what the trouble was. The organisation of the picture had certainly gone wrong; half the galloping horses were resolutely facing one way, and half the other. Exasperated children were pushing the cut-outs here and there in vain hope of making things come right. Among the cut-out riders was one very ambitious attempt by a ten-year-old boy to depict a horse front view, leaping head-on towards him. An intelligent girl saw that this figure could resolve their difficulty. Seizing a piece of chalk, she sketchily indicated the lines of a barbed-wire fence on the background paper. In the fence she put a gate, and then placed the front-view, leaping horse behind the gate, apparently just taking off to jump it. In the field behind the fence, the horses with their heads turned towards the right galloped towards the gate: in

87

front of the fence those with their heads turned to the left galloped furiously away from it after the fox now strategically placed in the bottom left-hand corner. The effect of the 'accident' was to fill the picture with story value, and to arrange a much better composition than had at first been conceived.

Later that week, the infants were given their share of this picture, being employed to cut out and colour leaves of varying shapes, sizes and colours to be stuck on the trees, hedges and bushes. Two little boys of six were cutting leaves for a very large tree, and had elected to paint them a brilliant crimson, as the knowledgeable boys in the upper group had made it known that fox-hunting did not take place in spring or summer. The leaves having been cut out first, they had to be held down by the small fingers of the left hand while the paint was applied. Again there was consternation at the discovery of little finger-marks in the wet paint, and again the imagination of a six-year-old saved the day. He deliberately patterned the leaves all over with the tips of his tiny fingers, producing such a beautiful broken pink and crimson texture that the tree immediately took on a true artistic life of its own.

It is obvious that the 'stick on' method of co-operative work has a great deal to commend it from many points of view. This is especially true when materials other than straightforward paint or crayon are being used.

I go more fully into some of the ways of picture-making other than straightforward painting on p. 149, but for the moment I shall continue with media for that.

Paint and Crayon

Powder colour has proved its worth, and for bold results and economy it cannot be beaten, but it is by no means the only colour medium for children to use. However, since it is by far the most common, I will deal with it first. The quality that makes powder tempera so popular is its versatility. It can be used thick, stiff and opaque, or thin and semi-transparent. It mixes well and produces good tones and tints. The children must be encouraged to use this versatility and to explore all the possibilities of this paint. It should be given to them dry, so that they can mix it according to their needs. The nine-hole bun tin is the best container I have ever found, as this gives just the right range of colour. My tins usually contain the following: cobalt, crimson, vermilion, gamboge, viridian, black, white, raw and burnt umber. With these nine colours almost any shade is possible. (Always remember when ordering that white is needed with practically every picture, and at least twice as much white as any other colour is used; similarly, all the yellows are 'soft' colours, and go more quickly, so it is advisable to order an extra tin or two of this, too.)

The other absolute necessity is a palette of some kind to mix on. It is a sheer waste of money to buy the tiny palettes we used to use with watercolour in our schooldays. Practically any flat, smooth, non-absorbent surface will do. I have sandwich tins (enamelled once a year), biscuit tin lids: plastic plates and saucers (and old china ones too), slabs of thick glass and oddments of asbestos cut from bath panels, etc., given to me by a friendly plumber.

I have heard many complaints from teachers about giving the children powder paint dry, mainly on two grounds: (a) that it gets spilt too easily, and (b) that it is difficult to store bun tins full of dry powder.

To (a) I answer that it is easier to clean up dry powder than mixed paint, especially from a polished floor. Never throw away the queer mixture that you sweep up: keep empty tins on purpose to store it, for the chances are that before the month is out someone will want exactly the colour that the strange mixture has made. We had quite a store of such inadvertently mixed colours, and everybody, including the unfortunate children who spilled it, joined in the joke when the wit of the class carefully labelled the tins according to the offender's name, 'Beverly grey' or 'Philip blue', etc., so that they could be easily identified for future use.

The other point is also very easily dealt with; simply stack the bun tins in the cupboard alternately, one straight and the other diagonally across it. The cups do not then sit into each other, no paint is flattened and the bottoms of the tins are kept clean.

One bun tin per group of four children should be enough if the desks can be arranged that way: one tin to two children is luxury.

If there are still those who cannot face the dry powder method, then it is possible to use other things with equally good results. The tempera can be bought in tins already mixed, called 'liquid tempera'. The mixture is fairly thick and can be thinned, but never can one get the lovely feeling of 'bite' of brush on paper that is experienced with dry powder mixed to a stiff paste. Liquid tempera is not for me, but it may suit others perfectly. A much better medium than the mixed powder in my estimation is 'temperapaste'. This is really delightful. It is made by many firms, and can be bought in anything from 2 ounce tubes to 7 pound jars. The paste itself resembles oil paint, and can be used with effect, stiff and sticky as one would use oils, but it can also be thinned down to a transparency only excelled by true watercolour. The colours are clear and brilliant, and to me their only drawback is that one cannot leave the palette ready for use from one lesson to the next, as one can with the tins of powder, because the paste dries hard and cannot be re-used except for very thin washes. It becomes absolutely necessary, therefore, on grounds of economy, to train the children to help themselves *only* to the amount they think they will use up, and as there is always the careless and the greedy child in every class, some paint will inevitably go down the sink at the end of the lesson. One must be realistic about this waste of paint, or of whatever material is being used. It really depends on what you mean by 'waste'. All experience has to be paid for in some way or other, and a little paint down the sink is no more to get upset about than an exercise book full of spelling mistakes, or incorrect sums, though most teachers would regard these as inevitable, and would hardly stop to worry about the waste of paper and ink. The real waste would be in time and energy if the children in question never improved in number-work or English. Similarly, the real waste of paper and paint in the art class occurs in the heap of unrecognisable, soggy, wishy-washy pictures that are picked up at the end of so many art lessons. One cannot say that materials that produce good results are wasted if a little too much is taken, but a term's issue of art materials can be utterly thrown away if the children are no better at the end of the term, and no happier in using them, than they were at the beginning.

So far I have talked exclusively of paint, but there are many other media with which to provide colour. Wax crayons are my second choice—both the big fat 'free art' and the smaller 'fine art' crayons should be in every art cupboard. Many children have cheap watercolour boxes of their own that they use incorrectly at home, thereby undoing a great deal of the good the freedom of the school art lesson has done. They are usually willing to bring these boxes to school with them, and can then be taught how to use them skilfully in pen-and-wash technique, for real watercolour painting is a very specialised art and needs really good materials. Coloured inks are a strange and exciting medium and lend themselves to fine work with squirrel-hair brushes. Charcoal and chalk are invaluable for sketching bold outlines before painting, and some children simply delight in the contrast of using them together, with no other colour added. Then there are the coloured pencils, especially the soft, square-ended ones so useful for teaching italic writing, either black, or in a good range of colours.

I know that such a variety of materials costs money in the first place, but common sense insists that the children cannot be using all of them at once, and that over an academic year there is very little difference in cost if smaller quantities of several things are used instead of a large quantity of one thing.

While on the subject of the colour medium, I must emphasise the need to use that freely, too, while the supply lasts, and to ignore the cost. I am not forgetting the limits of the annual requisition allowance, nor can I suggest any magic way of making it go further. All I can do is to offer advice on how to use the materials it will buy. The experience gained by using paint properly will give the children the confidence they need to go on experimenting with the infinite variety of materials that can be had for nothing but the trouble of collecting them.

While the materials do remain, try the effect of mixing them. The results can be new and unexpected. Wax crayon super-imposed on powder paint often 'pulls the picture out'; paint washed over wax crayon gives a 'wax resist' which may be ideal for clouds, for instance. In similar ways wax crayon and coloured inks can be used; chalk and pastel with paint or ink, black ink with watercolour, etc., etc.

What has been said about quality of paper and paint applies equally to brushes. The better the quality of the brushes in the first place, the longer they will last, if proper care is taken of them. There should be different kinds to choose from, bristle and hair, of differing sizes, and shapes, that is, round, flat and filbert shaped. All brushes need care and should be well washed at the end of each lesson, smoothed back into shape and stood, bristle end up, in a jar. Even with all this care they are bound to show signs of feathering by the end of the term. The remedy then is simplicity itself. Wash them thoroughly, then dip each one separately in water into which a good tablespoonful of condensed milk has been mixed. Smooth the bristles back into shape and leave over the holidays. At the beginning of the next term the milk simply washes off, and the brush has been trained back into its original shape.

With the utmost care in the world, the brushes will wear out some day. Don't make the mistake of trying to go on using them when the bristles begin to fall out or break off, but don't throw them away, either. Keep them for the kinds of art work in which sticking is necessary—and they are legion. To sum up the question of materials, then, these basic principles apply: (*a*) buy *good* stuff, (*b*) look after your materials, (*c*) use them freely, and (*d*) don't be afraid to experiment.

PRESENTATION OF THE SUBJECT

On the many occasions when I have been actually talking to gatherings of other teachers about art in school and have reached this particular point, I have usually been aware of a discreet rustling (and jiffling) among my audience, and the next moment little note-books and pencils have appeared on almost every knee. I wait until all are settled again, and then boldly suggest that the little note-books be put away again, for disappointing though it may be, I do not propose to give them a long list of subjects suitable for next term's art lessons. It would, in the first place, be quite impossible for one teacher to prescribe for another's class, and in any case, what would be suitable for 1 *a* would not necessarily be suitable for 4 *c*. But the little note-books make me sad, for they suggest that while most teachers accept that they must take the art lesson anyway, whether they enjoy it or not, many of them panic at the

93

thought of having to suggest several subjects for painting during the term. That is one of the reasons why so many children, without the proper experience to call upon, are left to 'paint what they like'.

Children have a natural gift for expressing themselves in picture form, and if they have not been inhibited in any way, will draw and paint as naturally as they talk or move. However, this statement presupposes that the child *has* something to express, and that he is left in perfect freedom to express it how and when he likes. Every normal adult can talk, and put his thoughts into words; but confront any adult with a watch and say, 'When I say "Go", I want you to say as many words beginning with "B" as you can in one minute,——"Go".' Then watch the blankness that creeps into his eyes, the desperate efforts to collect his thoughts, the working of the lips and the clumsiness of the tongue trying to say a simple word like 'butter', if such a common, everyday word occurs to him at all. Much more usually it is words like 'bacciferous' or 'brachy-cephalic' that struggle to his tongue, and if you ask him afterwards why he found it so difficult he will usually say that the only words he could really think of were those not suitable for drawing-room games.

It is something of the same kind of blankness that comes over the mind of a child when it is told to 'paint what it likes'. There is a terrifying inability suddenly to select one particular thing from the mass of experience collected and absorbed since the previous day. Left completely isolated and unaided in this overwhelming sea of impressions, the child clutches at the first straw his mind throws up, which is too often something that he has found fairly safe before, or attempts something that some well-meaning but misguided adult has 'shown him how to do'. We all know the result—the endless repetition of the square house with the window at each corner, the smoke from the central chimney always blowing the same way, the 'match-stick' tractor, the toffee-apple trees, and the minute, static train. However careful in execution such pictures may be, surely no teacher can delude himself into thinking that they are either 'art' or 'self-expression'. Such works bear absolutely no relation to the colourful daubs, the soggy messes, the unintelligible splodges that are produced by the same children in a free-activity period which, if properly conducted, has left them completely free. Free, that is, to ignore paint in favour of some other activity if they so wish, but if they choose paint, then free to explore it and to experiment with it and to 'express themselves' in it without contamination by adult interference of any kind. Such experience is invaluable, and in speaking of the art lesson in the junior school, one hopes that one may pre-suppose a wealth of that kind of experience in the infant school.

From such exploration grows a confidence that may enable certain children to plunge straight in without hesitation when told that they may paint what they like, especially when the materials before them are as varied and enticing and the atmo-sphere as free as when they were in the infant school: but if this alone were enough, there would be no need for art teachers, or indeed for this book at all. One can bring a horse to water, but one cannot make him drink. The art teacher can only do his best to bring his pupils to the stream of knowledge and pleasure thirsting for it, and uninhibited by any fear of drowning.

To return to the subject for the art lesson. It is equally un-rewarding to suggest to the class that they 'illustrate a story'. Again, the prospect is too wide. The mind is presented with a panorama in which no single landmark stands out. How can one possibly illustrate the story of Cinderella, for instance, in one lesson, or even in one afternoon? Only too well do those who have tried it know the results of this kind of approach, the frantic, despairing attempts to get in everything in the story, from the mice and the pumpkin to the two ugly sisters and the wedding coach, or else the badly executed attempts to reproduce the ugly, or pretty-pretty illustrations of Walt Disney and his less able imitators, remembered almost against the will from some cheap fairy story book.

The search for the right kind of subject is primarily the teacher's responsibility, but once a few basic principles are accepted, the responsibility is light and the search so interesting that it becomes a pleasure in itself. After a little while, one finds that wherever one's eyes turn, whenever one's ears catch an unexpected sound, whenever the mind accepts the full meaning of a descriptive phrase, there is the subject for a picture. Under the influence of a teacher alert and receptive himself, it is not long before the children are just as aware as he is, and the cry of 'Wouldn't that make a lovely picture?' is the last stage before the final one, that of the instinctive, spontaneous rush to the paint cupboard of children who know truly what paint is for, and the absorbing thrill of being able to use it to catch the beautiful flying moments of the present before they disappear for ever into the past.

A picture catches a moment in time, whether it portrays the stillness of a vase of flowers or the multitude of people leaving a football ground. It cannot deal with a period of time, it can only make one moment in time timeless. To ask a child to 'illustrate the story of Cinderella' is to ask it to record a story which takes place in time. Walt Disney and his team of draughtsmen did this by making the still moments overlap, but we cannot, even if we would, imitate him in school. So if we want a picture from the story of Cinderella, we must set about getting it in ways which are possible and reasonable to us. The first thing is to 'pin-point' the moment we want to catch. Then 'illustrating a story' immediately becomes a possibility. Choose several scenes from the story, and hold them up to the children in a frame so to speak. Make them try to see just the scene you want them to see, in detail, and nothing else. Ask them to close their eyes and *think* the picture. Cinderella herself, for instance, crouched in her rags beside the dying fire on the hearth. Nothing else, not even the mantelpiece with an array of ornaments. Cinderella bringing the mousetrap to the fairy godmother. Can we show two full length human figures in this scene with success? Obviously not, for if we tried, the mousetrap and the mice would be reduced to such minute proportions as to be completely unrecognisable. Moreover, the chances are that the fairy godmother would be felt as a pantomime fairy, all wings and tinsel and no character, saying nothing to anyone, not even to her creator. This is a subject for close-up treatment, with the heads and hands only of Cinderella and the godmother as they bend over the trap of white mice. A scene like this is so easily dramatised that it will take no more than five minutes of the lesson to show the rest of the class two heads bending over two hands holding the chalk-box, or something equally handy, to represent the mousetrap. Imagination will do the rest.

If you want to use scenes from everyday life, use exactly the same method. 'Mother in the kitchen' would probably produce a picture bespattered with cooking stoves and refrigerators and vacuum cleaners and sink units, with a microscopic blob that you guess is mother. 'Mother making a pudding' narrows the vision down to a paintable size, and again, a quick bit of dramatisation will show the intelligent children that perhaps the picture need include nothing of mother below table level, and that the bowl and the spoon are paintable in their own right. 'Changing the wheel' does not need to be a landscape with a stamp-sized car, nor does it want to be a picture of a special make of car suitable for an advertisement, however much the painter is interested in the make of the car. The crouching figure adjusting the wheel, with his head, at the level of the mudguard touching the top of the paper (or very nearly) and his feet the bottom, is enough. So with street scenes, so with sports scenes, so with any scene.

Illustrating a poem needs the same touch, too. Take a poem like Harold Munro's *Milk for the Cat* for instance, which is found in most school anthologies. Here is a poem with nine four-lined stanzas, and though it is all about a cat, a closer study of it will show that it portrays the same cat in no less than seven distinctly different feline attitudes. Now though a child may register each of these attitudes as something known and loved from his knowledge of cats in general as the poem proceeds, the impression left with him at the end of the poem is just 'cat', and though a closer study of the poem as poetry may serve to make him appreciate the poet's observation of a cat, to ask simply that he paint a picture of the cat in the poem is still asking for trouble. He will not know what to choose, even if he had thought consciously of the cat in each of the attitudes, which is not really very likely. It is ten chances to one that the picture would either turn out to be a cypher cat drawn in circles, remembered from some book of trick drawings, or a nondescript four-legged animal which could just as easily be taken for a cow or a dog. The essential cattiness of the poem will not be attempted. If, however, two or three attitudes are 'pin-pointed' for him, the child will immediately find that he has a wealth of observation of his own stored up to help him.

> The white saucer like some full moon descends
> At last from the clouds of the table above;
> She sighs and dreams and thrills and glows,
> Transfigured with love.
>
> She nestles over the shining rim,
> Buries her chin in the creamy sea;
> Her tail hangs loose; each drowsy paw
> Is doubled under each bending knee.

Either of these two stanzas makes a perfect picture in itself. The first is particularly good, because the scale of the painting is set immediately by the saucer being likened to the moon, in the sky of the picture, as it were, so that it is quickly understood that the figure putting down the saucer is not required, though the hand carefully lowering it may be necessary to explain it. Having got the saucer and the hand, the size of the cat is merely relative, and as this must now be of necessity almost large enough to fill the rest of the paper, it is obvious that the details of the cat must be thought about and portrayed. Here the experience of their own cats comes to the children's aid, and they begin to sketch in the cat rubbing herself in ecstasy against the table leg, her eyes on the saucer, or rising on to her hind legs to push her nose against the saucer in that exasperating way that cats have which always results in the milk being spilt before they ever get it.

Similarly the second stanza describing the cat actually drinking is narrowed so successfully that a close-up of the cat is accepted without question. To take one further example, let us choose one suitable for town children. (I am very often told that the country children have all the advantages in finding subjects to paint.) Here is John Drinkwater's poem about the blackbird.

> He comes on chosen evenings,
> My blackbird beautiful, and sings
> Over the gardens of the town
> Just at the hour the sun goes down.
> His flight across the chimneys thick
> By some divine arithmetic,
> Comes to his customary stack
> And couches there his plumage black,
> And there he lifts his yellow bill,
> Kindled against the sunset, till
> These suburbs are like Dymock woods

Where music has her solitudes,
And while he mocks the winter's wrong,
Rapt on his pinnacle of song,
Figured above our garden plots,
Those are celestial chimney pots.

As a poem this is much more difficult, but as a picture it is just as good. Once they have grasped the meaning of the poem, even the dullest will realise that they are being asked to paint a blackbird among the chimney pots of a town at sunset. If it is then pointed out to them that the bird has to be big enough to be able to show the yellow bill against the sunset, common sense will tell them that it will not be possible to include rows and rows of houses to represent the town, nor even the whole of the house on which the blackbird is sitting. There may still be those who want a whole sky-line full of chimney pots, but why not? It would make a good picture, and is quite possible, even if the bird is then reduced in size, and if the poem has stimulated this moment of vision, it has done its work well. Others will take a quick look out of the window and really see a chimney pot for the first time, though imagination may have to supply the bird and the sunset.

So with pictures from verbal descriptions—the odd little incident observed by one person and described to the others. (This is a very valuable lesson in speech and the use of words, too.) Let me again give examples. While standing one day at my kitchen sink, washing up, I saw through the window a robin investigating the skin of half a pomegranate that had been thrown out and had somehow or other come to rest in the tangled bottom of the old hedge bordering the garden. The wood of the hedge was twisted and gnarled with age, and everywhere it was laced together with the glossy dark green leaves of ivy. There among it lay the bright pomegranate, yellow and rosy crimson, resting obliquely on one side of the cut edge, with its little crown on the top showing sharp against a particularly beautiful ivy leaf. The robin hopped up to it and stood eyeing it, his head on one side, apparently making up his mind whether or not it was worth a trial as a tit-bit. Here was a gift for a picture, for the incident, small as it was, was too beautiful to be enjoyed by one person only, and too good to be lost without comment. On my return to school I told the children about it, and the paintings that came from it showed how vividly my words had conveyed the scene from my mind to theirs.

Good verbal description of objects in a still-life group is a good way of starting interest in painting objects at first, because the children seem not to fear the group of imagined objects, and only put into their picture what their mind suggests, rather than what they see; but once they realise how much fun painting objects can be, then there is nothing like having a group set up for them to 'have a go' at. I would not suggest that this is done very often in the primary school, but used occasionally it can make the children observe in detail, an accomplishment most valuable to them, and on which they can draw for help with actual technique in future imaginative work. It should not need saying that on the few occasions when still life is used as a subject for the lesson, the group must be attractive and well arranged. A ripe custard marrow and a jar of Virginia creeper on a gay tablecloth of pale blue linen might arouse a young painter to unexpected heights of endeavour and success, while the chalk-box and the blackboard duster thrown together on the teacher's ink-worn desk would probably get the treatment it deserved from a young artist, however much it might inspire an adult painter whose gimmick lay in only using greys and blues.

All the so-called 'information subjects': history, geography, science and nature study, scripture, and above all, literature, present an abundance of subjects with a two-way value; but for the sake of the art alone, impressions of everyday life are invaluable, for by attempting such pictures a child learns to observe, and by translating his observation as only he can, each individual makes his own comment on life, thereby turning mere picture-making into art.

APPRAISAL

This is by far the most difficult of my three headings on which to give practical advice.

When the young man held up before the class the character-less red ship on the wishy-washy green sea and called it 'good', he was doing his own class and the world of children's art in general a greater disservice than all his other mistakes put together could have done. All children are eager for their teacher's praise, and believe his taste to be infallible. If he is satisfied with any piece of work, then the children believe un-questioningly that that work must be of the right kind, and the goal towards which they must strive. So by being too easily satisfied, and allowing all the rest of the children to hear his praise of such a mediocre piece of work, he set up a whole range of false criteria.

It may perhaps be argued that he was indeed satisfied with the picture, that according to his lights and experience it was indeed good. This is then more unfortunate still, for it points him out plainly as a teacher who has never been to any trouble at all to study the subject he has undertaken to teach. In fact, his sub-sequent conversation on 'modern art' (it used to be called the 'new art', I remember) revealed only too well that he possessed the little learning which is such a dangerous thing. He had, I think, made the mistake so common in the teaching profession that in itself it is worth comment: he had never been able to dissociate the method by which he himself had been taught from the method by which he was trying to teach.

Our own schooldays remain with us so vividly that years of experience and practice in other schools never succeed in wiping them out of our minds. What a fundamental fact of education we touch upon here, and consideration of it should give all teachers pause. What we are teaching now will be no more 'right' in fifty years' time than were my tearful attempts to draw the coal scuttle thirty years ago; methods will go on changing, though the curriculum remain unchanged for ever. This sobering thought should serve to remind us that neither what we teach nor any prescribed method of teaching it is ot much importance in itself. The things that really matter are that because of *what* we teach the children become interested enough to go on wanting to know; and that because of *how* we teach, and the example we present to them, the children should be able to think for themselves and have confidence in their own judgement. The two aspects of education put together will enable our charges to keep abreast of current ideas to the end of their lives. I have no doubt that Mr X had been brought up, even as I was, on 'drawing' with a pencil. Perhaps he was quite good at it, and gained a false idea of his own ability to teach art from his teacher's comments. Then while he was at college he heard of the new freedom in art, and as a 'method' he had to learn about it. It is obvious that he never really accepted it, nor perhaps even understood it. All he gathered were a few unrelated facts, such as that one now allowed children to use paint direct instead of pencil, that such things as perspective and 'shading' were now of no importance; that if a child wished to draw raindrops as big as turnips then that was quite acceptable and one must never interfere, and so on. Then he simply grafted the little knowledge he had gained of the 'new art' on to his own rather rigid experience, and in doing so fell fairly and squarely between the two stools. A picture of a ship, executed in line, with pencil or pen on suitable paper, could have been good from any point of view; so could a brilliantly crimson ship boldly painted in mass on a roaring green sea, if the child had chosen those colours himself, deliberately, from a wide palette. The mixture of the two was not acceptable, and if I must be pinned down to saying why, I can only answer that it was not *natural*. It had nothing in it of the nature of the medium, nor of the subject, nor of the artist; therefore it was not art.

There can surely be very few teachers now who have not heard or read of the modern methods in art, nor seen one of the ubiquitous exhibitions by means of which certain newspapers and artists' suppliers have tried to 'cash in' on the new movement. It has been going for so long now that it can hardly be called new any longer, and it is quite time that teachers understood what they were trying to do. Unfortunately it has been my experience that they have been trying very hard to do it without understanding it in the least. They have interpreted the word 'freedom' to mean that anything will do so long as it is unhampered by any rules. This, of course, is not freedom, but anarchy, and it has been fairly well established that in any field anarchy does not produce much worth while with the rank and file, however well it may suit the temperament of some great artists. Splashing about with paint and water may be no more art than drawing a laurel leaf with a 2H pencil.

It is not my business here to write about the theory of the newer method—for one thing many more capable people have done it already, from Cizek and Viola onwards. Every teacher should, however, be able to understand the fundamental principle of the change: that before the new movement it was the adult conception of what art was that was applied to the child, who was taught to draw in adult techniques, to represent objects as pictorially accurate as possible. What objects were drawn mattered not at all, nor whether the results gave pleasure to anyone, so long as the technique was good. Thus, when the Society for the Diffusion of Useful Knowledge sponsored a little book called *Drawing for Young Children* in 1838, the author wrote a preface which told clearly of his great knowledge of a child's powers of observation, reasoning and understanding, and even of the limitations of children's ability to draw accurately. This latter however, said he, could be cured by constant practice; and he went on to suggest that the child should copy, not from the actual object, but from the simplified sketch he himself had thoughtfully appended, 'at least six times' before proceeding to attempt the same object from memory. 'But', he adds in his instructions to the teacher, 'the greatest care must be taken not to disgust him [the pupil] by too much sameness, or to render him heedless by too frequent change'. The first six objects are then presented:

(1) A butcher's block   (4) An extinguisher
(2) A milestone   (5) A cleaver
(3) A knife   (6) A bird's head

One may be excused for thinking that if it were the generation of young people we know that was being introduced to such objects, we might be thankful that they were only to do them from copies, and not from 'nature', for they would undoubtedly find other uses for the knife, the cleaver and the butcher's block rather than to draw them.

With all his knowledge of children, the author of this little book applied only his adult technique, and only a very few steps had been taken forward by the time I received my primary education. All that had happened was that because it had been recognised that children loved colour, the pencilled outlines could now and then be filled in, to make the lesson more interesting, not to produce better art.

The new conception of child art simply takes into account that children are not solely adults in the making, but creatures in their own right, as tadpoles differ from mature frogs, or caterpillars from butterflies. They have their own set of emotions, abilities, and techniques. What is expected of them is child-like, not pre-adult work. All that is asked is that they should do what comes naturally to them, within the bounds of reason and common sense.

This never has meant that 'just anything' will do in art, any more than a set of figures printed upside down and back-to-front would be called a sum and accepted as such for very long, in the arithmetic lesson, though many children write their number symbols the wrong way round at first. In the early stages of number, as long as they understand the threeness of three, so to speak, the printing of the symbol backwards is of small moment, but the teacher usually tries her hardest to persuade a child that there is a right way round before he leaves the infant school. Similarly, in art, the figure with the arms coming out directly from the side of the head would be completely acceptable from a four-year-old, because of the moment of vision behind the attempt to portray a man: but to allow a normal child of eleven to draw a man like this on the grounds that it was 'child art' would be a piece of conscious naïveté that would turn the stomach of a sincere artist or teacher. So while we do not now impose adult standards, we work towards them as the child grows towards adulthood, which really means that all children go on developing naturally, and that the development should show in the work they produce.

It is therefore absolutely imperative for any teacher that he possess criteria of his own, and that because they can trust his judgement, his pupils can learn to form their own. He must have standards, and they must be high. In applying them he is bound to be critical, and fails in his duty if he is not. The teacher who smiles encouragingly at every unrecognisable daub and tells the perpetrator that it is good, just to encourage him, must expect nothing better, for as Dr Johnson so rightly said, he who praises everybody praises nobody. In fact, this teacher may often expect worse, especially from an intelligent class, for I would not put it beyond any boy I had in my recent class, under such influence, to put his tongue into his cheek and try deliberately to see just how far he could go. Most children instinctively mistrust this kind of fulsome flattery, and know, as country people say of a frozen potato, that it is 'oversweet to be wholesome'.

Nor are children averse to candid criticism provided that it is honest, fair and constructive. Moreover, they are the very best critics of each other's work, and once trained well, of their own. The boy or girl who always says 'I don't like mine' is the most dangerous, for he is usually courting flattery from his teacher and his fellows: but the child who will stand before his own picture now and then and say 'I think mine is the best' has proved his confidence in himself not only as an artist, but as an unbiased critic.

In being critical, however, the teacher must not avoid Scylla only to fall a victim to Charybdis. However good the children are, they will not produce adult work. Their work will be essentially child-like, and to assess this work anyone is up against a very real difficulty. For though he was a child himself once, though he may have made a serious study of child psychology and development, though he may have spent years at work among children, the fact is inescapable that he is an adult now. His memories of childhood are remembered with an adult memory, his knowledge of children is an adult's knowledge, and his conception of what is child-like is adult, too. The absolutely impossible thing for most people is to see anything as a child sees it, unclouded by maturity, and not through the mirror of assimilated experience. So in being critical he must beware of judging by what *he thinks* a child should do, or what a child should like; the criterion is what the child does do, and what he likes. The ability to turn again to childhood and see the world truly through childish eyes is given to very few men, though among them we number some of the literary geniuses of our language. The absence of this ability, on the other hand, accounts for a good deal of the nauseating whimsy found in story books for children and the illustrations that decorate them.

Whimsy is 100 per cent adult: when a small child peoples its imaginative world with cats or horses, this is not whimsy, but anthropomorphism. When an adult uses his knowledge of this anthropomorphic tendency in children in order to 'play down' to their level, the result is, more often than not, sickeningly whimsical. The works of the few men who have truly been able to return to the child's world have become classics. They include such men as Lewis Caroll, Kenneth Grahame, and even, perhaps, A. A. Milne. It is an interesting thought that the works of these men are as interesting to and popular with grown-ups as children: for while they enter directly the child's anthropomorphic world at one level, they enter the adult world at another, holding, as they do, a kind of satirical mirror to mankind showing us our own idiosyncrasies and human failings through the animal characters. We all have met and know the bombastic Toads and humble Rattys of life, the officious White Rabbits, self-satisfied and pedantic Owls, timid Piglets, lugubrious Eeyores, and one-track-minded mother Kangas.

These old favourites cannot be classed as whimsy, but the endless reiteration of rabbits in rompers and bunnies in buster suits and pussies in pinafores and doggies in dinner jackets *ad nauseum* is unendurable. It has become a feature of some of the newer reading schemes, often to the exclusion of the real folk-tale, but for goodness' sake let us keep it out of the art lesson.

The teacher who has a slick gift for perpetrating little Mickey Mouses (or should one say Mickey Mice) and leaves evidence of this gift decorating cupboard doors and register covers should at least be moved to teaching Physical Education or Mathematics, where he cannot be quite such a danger.

The teacher who cannot draw at all should refrain from trying in front of his class, though experiment will soon teach him that painting and drawing are not the same thing. I am reminded of the tale told me by an old friend of mine, who was about to take a lesson on the Sahara Desert. She spent a valuable dinner time trying to draw a camel on her blackboard. When the children returned to their seats, they gazed stolidly at the picture, and finally one of them volunteered, 'I've got one o' them at 'ome'. This is what the teacher had been hoping for, a direct approach to her lesson. 'Ah,' she said, 'and what is it?' Back promptly came the answer. 'Please Miss, a Loch Ness monster.'

Yet I have seen a painting of a jam jar of leaves and berries done by the same teacher for a nature class that was breathtaking in its feeling.

The best assessors of what is right for a certain age group are the children in that age group. The teacher should endeavour to learn from his children what kind of work to expect, and it is then up to him to see that such work is produced at the highest level of quality, and that the children progress, reaching always forward and upward, but still with their feet on ground they feel to be safe. Part of this ground is their trust in their teacher's ability to understand what it is they are attempting, and then to give his judgement freely without fear or favour, affection or ill-will, being neither too hard to please, nor too easily satisfied.

There are always one or two 'born' artists in every class, and the other children will be quick to recognise and appreciate this gift in their peers: but at the other extreme there will also be those whose attempt at painting David slaying Goliath will look like a greasy pudding-bag picked up from a field on a muddy day. These children must always be given their mead of encouragement. In selecting pictures for display on the wall, for the head teacher's room, etc., the good teacher will remember that it is really his job to give *all* his children some confidence in themselves, and not merely to provide 'eye-wash' for visitors. The clever child artist will have rewards in plenty, by the sheer virtue of his work and his own inner satisfaction; and the less able child will get the thrill of his life and an incentive to better work ever after if he occasionally sees one of his works displayed, for with art as with everything else from slimming to big business, nothing succeeds like success.

NATURAL DEVELOPMENT

It would be so much easier to write this section if I could refer my readers to one picture after another to exemplify the points I want to make, as I can when lecturing; but I know that the number of pictures I can hope to have reproduced must be small, and that being so, I can only rely upon my readers to be discerning enough to recognise examples of the kinds I shall mention from amongst the work their own pupils produce.

For me to be able to see the natural development, in all its stages, of children between the ages of five and eleven is easy, because I have had children of that age range in my own hands all the time. It is much more difficult in a larger school where the children are divided into classes, and have teachers of varying ability and enthusiasm. Nevertheless, it would surely be worth any head teacher's time and trouble to make a collection of work done throughout his school during any one term, with the express object of being able to study the gradual development of perception and executive skill, and to serve as a rough guide and a criterion for each individual teacher, in showing him what it is reasonable to expect from the children of his particular class's age.

Paint has now been accepted almost everywhere as a necessity in the infant school, at any rate, but it would still puzzle a great many teachers to state why they think a small child wants or needs to paint. In the first instance, it seems to be that he desires simply to explore the new substance set before him. There is no doubt that a bun tin of brightly coloured powder colour is attractive, even to an adult, and a sheet of clean white paper promotes the same desire to stamp it with one's own individual mark as does a fresh expanse of newly fallen snow. To a child this impulse is irresistible. Water is an added stimulus, and first attempts at 'painting' are usually no more than straightforward trials to find out what happens. The very young child simply grabs his paint brush round the middle in a 'boy's grip', stabs it into the water, jabs it into the paint, and proceeds to scrub it round and round on the paper in a circular movement. He then repeats the whole process with colour after colour, till the paper is reduced to a soggy mess that has to be scraped from the desk or floor. This is an exploratory stage which is invaluable to the child in his understanding of the new and exciting medium he has discovered. It must be accepted and understood as such by his teacher, who should be prepared for it. It is bound to be heavy on paper, paint and patience, but it is as important to the structure of the child's artistic development as the digging of the foundations is to a house. One can only begin to think in terms of beautiful chimneys when the rest of the house is built.

This stage may continue for a few days only, or it may go on for weeks. It depends on other factors, such as the innate intelligence of the child, external stimuli, the atmosphere of the school, and so on. But sooner or later will come the day when from the mess of paint and water there emerges some kind of pattern. It may be noticed first, perhaps, in the separating of the colour, red and blue and yellow and green now being laid side by side instead of on top of each other: or in the different movement of the brush, which may now be used vertically and horizontally as well as spirally. This pattern again soon changes to another, which often contains the beginnings of texture, paint being applied in spots or 'dabs' in some places. At this point there is such a similarity in the patterns produced by children that it is in itself worth comment. If analysed, it will often be found that these patterns contain much the same elements, a large circular shape or spiral, flanked by a vertical shape, or two uprights, and the circle is more often than not decorated by dabs and spots. It may be, as has been suggested to me, that this is really a first attempt at drawing a human figure, conceived as a round head and either a vertical trunk or two vertical legs, while the spots represent the eyes, nose, and mouth. I am prepared to believe this, for I have had enough evidence to convince me that what the tiny hands succeed in putting on paper at this stage bears very little resemblance to the image in the young mind as the child paints. It may make no sense at all to a grown up, but the young imagination is so strong that the child sees on his paper what he is thinking, not what he has drawn. So, once complete confidence in his teacher has been established, a child to whom words come easily may interpret for her a completely unintelligible mass of splodges and squiggles and holes scrubbed in the paper as 'a man who is ever so cross because the wheel has come off his car and he has crashed into a tree'.

The next stage reached is that of real pictorial representation, and it is my experience that this stage is often reached as a result of a fortuitous accident. In using his paint and brush in experimental fashion, the child produces a pattern which bears some resemblance to something he recognises as part of his environment, and in delight he realises that he has 'made a tree', or any similar object. Then, having discovered for himself that objects around him can be thus represented, he goes on trying consciously to produce things he sees as well as those originating in his creative, fertile mind. It should be obvious to the most insensitive adult that this is the right way for him to learn, and that though his picture of a tree may in no detail accord with his teacher's concept of the same thing, it is *his own*, and is infinitely preferable to a more easily recognisable one that his teacher has 'shown him how to do'.

When his foot has once been firmly placed on this rung of the ladder, there is no stopping his ascent, and the chances are that before many days he will come rushing out of his place, bearing a picture in which, for instance, there are two objects vaguely resembling human beings, and shouting excitedly, 'Look. Look. I've drawed me and my mum in the garden'. The first platform in his general education has been reached, because from now onwards he can use his ability to draw and paint as a means of expression for his ideas. This is a valuable acquisition, for it comes between the use of the spoken and the written word in most children's development, and if seized upon can be a most useful asset to the teaching of English. (Much more about this later.)

Now he can press forward into painting as an art. The stage described above is usually over by the time the child reaches the mental age of six, and we are now about to consider the development of children from the age of six upwards. The years of real infancy have been used to adjust the child to his environment, without, perhaps, his having become particularly aware of it. From about six onwards he not only sees, but understands what he sees. Let us think for a moment of a cat as a part of an infant's environment. When the child is very young, his interest in a cat is probably mainly tactile—it is simply a bundle of fur which is nice to feel. As his understanding develops, he knows it as something which moves and makes a noise; that is, he is now able to recognise it visually and aurally. When he begins to walk, it is something with which to experiment, to pick up, to carry about, to make cry out. Soon it can be recognised as 'a cat', named, picked out in pictures, and so on. Such responses as have been made to this object in his life are so far physiological, that is for instance, pleasure at the softness of the fur, or pain and fear if scratched. It is not until the child has developed much further mentally that other, more complex responses such as admiration, love, possession and companionship are aroused. This I believe to be true as a general principle, that children know and accept their environment before they offer any emotional response to it: but that the clearer they see it, the better they know it, and that the more they know it, the greater will be their response.

In guiding the children towards this awareness of their surroundings, the practice of art plays a great part. To begin on a purely practical level, the attempt to reproduce any well-known object has the effect of making the child look closer, of training the 'seeing eye'. This alone, of course, would not be art, though it might add to skill in pictorial representation. Art demands some response from the artist. 'Emotion' is a dangerous word, and I am not suggesting that children should paint simply to 'express', or, to quote Mr T. S. Eliot, 'turn loose' their emotions, though there may, of course, be odd occasions when there is need for exactly that, when to paint will help a child to 'square up' to some overwhelming occurrence in his life. This is not, however, what I mean at the moment. What I am trying to say is that the total experience of a cat, for instance, includes something more than that gained by vision, hearing, or touch; and the something more is that which comes from the spirit. It is the projection of this part of the experience which turns drawing into art, words into poetry, melody into music. Into a real work of art goes something of the artist, though it may neither 'turn loose' an emotion, nor 'express' his personality. The urge to *do something* about a specific experience is the real germ of art.

A little time ago, I happened to be ill for a few days, and the only supply teacher the L.E.A. could find at short notice was an Indian teacher who was staying nearby. She was a breath of new life to my children, and they enjoyed the short change enormously. She told them a great deal about life in India and, on the last day that she was with them, brought for them to see a magnificent tiger's skin, with the head faultlessly preserved in all its savage beauty. When I went into school to thank her on this day, it was hanging across my desk, facing the class, and the children were gazing entranced at it, though with a variety of expressions on their faces. The next day, when I returned, the familiar atmosphere of my presence loosed their tongues, and they talked excitedly about it. I knew that it was inevitable that it would inspire some kind of art, and I was not wrong.

Angelo, a gifted little Italian, had observed it with a practised 'seeing eye', which had recorded for him the actual details of the beauty of the skin. From his memory of it he painted a most realistic tiger, true to colour, texture, grace, magnificence. Philip, normally far less clever artistically than Angelo, had felt more than he had seen. He had been sitting directly in front of the head as it lay across my desk, and his picture was of a tiger charging head on towards him, eyes glaring and teeth laid bare, through a jungle of tall, tawny grass. But it was Avril who was the real artist, that day: Avril, who had poor vision and constant ill-health, and exceedingly poor manual control. She left the paint to those who felt more at home with it, but the experience had been so strong that in spite of herself, almost, she was moved to record it. Her choice of medium was words, in which she felt able to translate the feeling that had been stirred within her. Her poem was a work of pure art.

A Tiger's Skin

A tiger's skin is orange
With black stripes on its back.
Its tail is black with white on too.
It looks as if it really is a tiger.

But you can stroke it,
And it will not hurt you at all.
You can feel right in its mouth,
And it cannot bite you.

This is as it should be. There is a continuous growth of artistic skill and technique at this stage, and with it should come the courage to experiment in new and unusual media.

To see the gradual development of artistic skill and the growth of the artistic spirit, it is necessary and most interesting to look at the work of one particular child over a period of years, and at the work of a group of children of ages varying from five to eleven, all attempting the same thing at the same time.

Jill was the youngest member of a family of five children who lived practically opposite the school. Two of her older sisters were in the school, and by the time Jill was three it was quite usual for me to look up and find Jill there, too, sturdy, fat, and firm, fair as ripe corn and with enormous eyes the colour of cornflowers. Whatever the others did, Jill attempted, and when paint came out, Jill painted with the rest. Her first artistic 'messes' it was impossible to keep, but so absorbed was she in the process that I kept watch for the signs of the development I expected. Before she was three and a half she was separating her colours and controlling her brush. At three and a half the spots and dots gave way, one morning, to two flower-like shapes side by side, fitting perfectly into the oblong paper she had chosen. Then the really great day arrived, when Jill was just four. The hounds met on our village green, right opposite the school. We all went out to watch the colourful scene, and on our return to school, with one accord made straight for the paint cupboard. Jill's picture was positive proof of the great step she had taken.

One of the creatures in her picture, seated on an undoubted quadruped of some sort, appeared to be turning a rope over his head. I stood above Jill as she painted on the floor, and bending down, pointed to it.

'What's this man doing, Jill?' I asked.

Like two bits of blue Delft her eyes turned up to me as she replied, with the lisp that in those days she had, 'He'th thkipping'. Somewhat surprised, I said, 'I didn't see anyone skipping on a horse'. With complete conviction she answered, 'Oh, didn't thyou? I DID.' It was not until the next time that I saw a hunt in full cry that I realised just how exact Jill's perception had been, and how, in the light of her own previous experience, she had conceived the notion of skipping: for having now seen the scene through Jill's eyes, so to speak, I too observed how very like skipping the combination of the reins and the bumping of the saddle could become.

At four and a half years she was painting 'out of her head', that is, from her own thoughts; the picture I kept she called, proudly, 'Me dancing'. The little dancing figure was quite recognisable, but what interested me most was the composition. Having set the figure too high in the paper, she boldly patterned with a line or two the space at the bottom, thereby at one stroke balancing her composition and making the dancing figure actually dance, for it was now leaping an inch or two above what must be taken to represent the floor. A series of imagina-

117

tive pictures followed, such as 'The witches house in the wood' and 'Fairies flying', none of them particularly remarkable, but all experimental. At five plus she joined some older children who were painting 'The judgement of Solomon'. There was Solomon in all his glory, wearing a cock-eyed crown and brandishing a Cossack's sabre, while in the other hand he held a pink, upside down human-like form, over which Jill was industriously painting a curious green shape. I was completely mystified, and curiosity overcame me.

'What's the green thing, Jill?' I asked.

Again the flash of blue as she answered, 'That'th the babith thun-thuit'. Here was another example of the child's immediate environmental experience being put to use side by side with her imagination. In her complete innocence Time did not exist, and Solomon had been brought right up to date.

Then it was that Jill, now about six, painted what has so far remained her masterpiece. Unasked, unaided, and completely unexpected, came 'A portrait of Mrs. Marshall doing her annual requisition'. The likeness, even to the hair-do, the grimace of concentrated calculation, the suggestion of futile exasperation and grim determination were all there, exactly as Jill must have remarked and comprehended me a day or two beforehand. With her picture, Jill was completely satisfied; with the same picture, I was entranced (plate 12).

It remained her masterpiece, as I have said, but for an unexpected reason. After showing all this amount of promise, she suddenly stopped painting. I was a little worried at first, but after a time I accepted the situation, and it was not long before the light of understanding broke upon me. She had begun to read very early, being quite fluent at five years, and by this time she had begun to write as well. Words were absorbing her, and paint offered nothing that words could not offer as well. Having realised what was happening, I was content to await developments of a new kind. Jill reached the great age of eight. Swans had somehow entered our lives, and several children had painted pictures in which swans formed the chief interest. There was still no real desire in Jill to paint, though she had recently co-operated with her cousin, Philip, in a large panel some five feet by two and a half feet depicting Jacob's Ladder, a magnificent piece of work with God at the top, complete with glaring, all-seeing eyes and a solar corona. But the swans had caught at Jill's imagination, and though she did not want to paint she needed an art to order this experience for her. She had a new art in her hands. At the end of the afternoon I had several pictures of swans on my desk, and this:

Swan

The swan comes gliding down the river,
Her black eyes like buttons,
Her red beak ruffling the water,
Her white fluffy feathers flapping gracefully.
Her black feet paddel behind her
As the water rippels past.
Her neck swoops down like an arch of snow,
And her reflection follows.

I have had many, many poems from children before and since this one, but never, I think, a better one, for it is, without doubt, the stuff of true poetry, made up, as Hopkins put it, of 'the very thew and sinew of the language'. From the age of about eight, Jill used one art as easily as the other. I doubt if she will go on painting or making puppets when she grows up; she may not even have occasion to do much writing; but she will assuredly go on talking, and her command of language is already great. She is now at a secondary modern school, and I am delighted to be able to report that very recently, at the age of twelve, she won outright a competition for public speaking held by the Young Farmers' Club, in the face of opposition from

119

girls and boys from the sixth form of local grammar schools; her subject, 'Hand-rearing pigs'!

This detailed study of the work of one child is often very salutary for the teacher, because in the context of education in general, it is far too easy for individual children to turn into that nondescript nonentity called 'the child'. It is so much more to the point of successful education to regard a class as a collection of individuals than to think of the individual children as fractions of a class. That is worth remembering when considering the second of my experiments to show how children develop artistically in the primary school years. When a whole group of children with ages ranging from four-plus to eleven-plus attempt the same picture, the various stages of perception and conception, skill and technique, development of emotional content, etc., can be seen as in a cross-section.

On two separate occasions I have asked all the children in the school to make a picture of themselves all playing the traditional singing game, 'Ring-a-ring-a roses'.

I gave them complete choice of paper and media, and noted down (a) their immediate reactions to my suggestion of the subject, (b) their choice of materials, (c) the time taken to complete the work to their own satisfaction, (d) any significant remarks made during the execution of the work, and (e) the resulting pictures.

When all the materials had been chosen and laid out ready to begin, we went into the playground and played the game for five minutes or so, before actually starting on the picture. I should like to be able to reproduce and comment on every single picture, for every one was a lesson in itself to any teacher. However, all I can do is to state the general findings of the experiment.

There were a few half-hearted groans of disapproval, mainly from the older children, when I first made the suggestion. The youngest made no demur whatsoever, though of course I knew that as a subject it was far beyond their executive skill. The protests came chiefly from the intelligent children, who perhaps realised how hard a task I was setting them, and who no doubt grudged the time to do something which had very little personal appeal to them.

Almost without exception, the children under seven and a half years chose either wax crayons or large 'Monk' pencils, while the older ones chose paint in either powder or tempera-paste. The smaller children took the smaller pieces of paper, while the older ones helped themselves to whole sheets of sugar paper, and in one or two cases requested pastel or cover paper (larger still), which I had neglected to put out ready.

The attack on the subject was direct and bold, with no hesitancy. Only two children seemed dubious as to their own ability, and both of these started two or three times on different pieces of paper, though they apparently repeated the same mistakes over and over again. This interested me very much, for though both children were of good average intelligence, whose art work was normally quite good, both had come to me from other schools after the infant stage, and it seemed that they lacked the confidence engendered by the early experience of paint in the infant school, and which the indigenous children had in plenty.

The time factor proved interesting, too. Most of the babies were difficult to time, for they would stop drawing and play for long periods, then suddenly seize a crayon and put in one or two lines with incredible swiftness before getting up and playing again. Even so, most of them had finished in twenty minutes, though I calculated that the actual drawing time for the youngest of all could not have been more than three to four minutes. The fives, sixes and sevens had all finished or given up before twenty-five minutes, and into this section also went older children of lower intelligence or who lacked perseverance. The work of the older children in this group did not lack artistic promise, but it seemed that their ideas were exhausted and that they had no will to finish what they had begun with confidence and enthusiasm. The eights, nines, tens and elevens who were left went on happily for an average of forty-five minutes, and the one or two who believed in doing a job really well went on for more than an hour. One boy frankly copied his neighbour, who happened to be a much younger child, and laid down his brush the moment that the smaller child did so; again, I found this most interesting, for I had known the child from the day he was born, and he was of more than average intelligence. But he was an only child who had been made an utter fool of, besides being frustrated in all the things a normal, lively boy wants to do. He was completely without tact, and often repeated to me what his parents had said about me, the school and his own relation to it. These remarks were often to the point that all this painting, etc., was a complete waste of time, that they were going to write 'to the Shire Hall' about it, and that the boy would do no good at all while he was at 'such a potty little school', but would 'get on when he was able to be one of a proper class', etc. In spite of all this, he was at heart a sensitive child with a gift for music and one who could, on occasion, produce nice art work. His copying on this occasion came, I knew, not from his lack of ability, but from deep-laid insecurity because he felt it impossible to be loyal to his parents and to me at the same time. He had read into my attitude the idea that I was particularly interested in what they were doing that afternoon, and therefore was not bold enough to tell me outright that he would not do what I asked; but to copy and to finish as soon as possible was as near to insurrection as he dared come. I saw all this happening, and guessed that he was expecting, and indeed, half hoping, for an outburst on my part that would give him something to take home for discussion, so of course I made no comment whatsoever on his work. Copying in art is almost unheard of in a class of children to whom painting is as natural as talking, and I am of the opinion that a child who habitually watches to see what others do before he starts has some inner problem to solve. The first thing that struck me about the actual pictures was that in spite of a dancing game being largely a question of movement, especially of leg movement, heads still remained the most important feature. Almost all the children started by drawing (I use the word to cover all methods of making shapes, whatever the medium) circles to represent the heads of the people playing the game. The few exceptions were the tiny children. They were, I think, utterly convinced that their pictures represented what they had been asked to portray, but it must be said at once that such representation existed only in the mind's eye. Two children of four-plus, Philip and Avril, sat side by side on the floor. Philip had one or two figures on his paper:

Avril had a number of crosses and circles executed sketchily in blue crayon, thus:

Philip, looking at Avril's work, said encouragingly, 'Draw the children playing, Avril'.

'I am', said Avril, putting in more blue crosses.

'She's not, is she?' said Philip to me.

'I AM', said Avril, before I could answer. 'These lines are the children.'

'Oo. They're not', said Philip scornfully. 'They're windows.'

Avril looked critically at her own work, then said (pointing to the circles), '*These* are the children, Philip.'

This shocked Philip into exclaiming, 'Oh. They're NOT. They aren't children, are they?' (appealing again to me).

Avril, obviously exasperated by this interference, shouted, 'I don't care. I like the windows best.'

Most of the five-year-olds showed a row of 'pin men' figures with heads much too large and arms growing out of their ears. I thought this rather strange, for I never draw or advocate the 'match-stick' man. In this age group there was practically no attempt at forming a circle of figures, but the line of figures was slightly curved towards the edges of the paper, as though the circle had actually been conceived, but only a part of it drawn because of the limitations of the paper.

At six-plus the ring of heads was usually completed, sometimes in an ellipse, which showed a fair amount of visual perception. When bodies and legs were added, however, they almost all turned inwards towards the centre of the ring; not one of the small artists remarked on this when their own or other's pictures were held up for them to see. It was quite plain that this arrangement of bodies and legs was as they saw it.

But at seven-plus there were several who had to experiment, and one who said to me that he 'didn't know where to put the feet of the people at the end', meaning those on the edges of the ellipse. After some thought, he put them outwards, though the other figures were vertical.

The eight-plus group's paintings were rather similar, but done in paint and on a larger scale. Up to this age all the faces of the ring of people had been done one way, that is facing the artist. Gay, an eight-year-old, saw her mistake when she held up her finished picture for me to see. She laughed and said, 'How daft. My children have got their backs to the ring—at least, these in the front have.'

The nines and tens were remarkable for the amount of detail that went into them. Boys and girls were now distinguishable, and some individuals recognisable by their long ginger plaits, startling red jerseys, and so on. The faces were now mostly turned inward, but most of the rings were quite static, and showed very little suggestion of movement, though several had figures with feet set wide apart, as in preparation for a dance to begin. Jean, eleven, remarked, 'These children aren't really playing, they are only standing in a ring'.

Only one child, Angelo (nine and a half), was able to bring off a picture in which children were really playing the game. In it his easily identifiable children were leaning towards the direction in which the game was travelling, with their legs in attitudes suggesting forward movement, heads tossing, arms swinging. Some children were elevated above ground level, springing forward in the dance. There was, over the whole ot his picture, a feeling of the joyous lightness, not only of feet but of heart, which is the essence of children at play.

To any teacher in doubt as to what can reasonably be expected of the children in his class I would suggest that he carries out one such experiment every term, and really takes trouble to study the results. He will learn a great deal, not about art, but about children. He will see (a) what a great part imagination plays in a small child's vision, (b) how actual visual perception develops gradually as the child grows older, (c) how long the average child of one particular age group can sustain his interest in one thing at one time, (d) at what age it is right to expect observation of detail, and (e) how a 'feeling' (call it an emotion if you like) entering into a picture can turn a mere drawing into real art.

⤙ 4 ⤚

The years of uncertainty were over. I still had much to learn, but there was no longer any doubt in my mind as to the value of what I was doing. I could go ahead now and experiment, put theory into practice, and even take risks without the tentative approach which always previously had suggested some slight uneasiness both as to the purpose and the result of any work undertaken.

As far as the visual arts were concerned, we had reached a standard of skill and proficiency which brought them at any moment into use as tools in skilled hands. From now onwards I proposed to get as much sheer pleasure out of creating pictures of all kinds and as many different media as possible; but I had never for a moment lost sight of 'the basic subjects', nor of the fact that to be 'educated' children must be given as wide a knowledge of the 'social subjects' as possible, nor that physical education is necessary to the overall pattern of growth and development, and that moral education should be based on some firm footing of belief.

Looking back on this stage of my life in the school, it is strange to me to see how at this point English, religious education (call it what you will), and art became inextricably mixed with each other. Because of the significance of this grouping of subjects, I shall not be able to deal at length with the other social subjects, but I hope I have said enough in the previous chapter to suggest that history, nature study and geography were by no means neglected in our schemes of work.

My main concern was with English. There are two ways of learning a foreign language. The first is by living among the people who speak it, as the armies of occupation learned German and Italian after the war; the other is to learn it from a grammar book, as in most grammar schools still, thereby becoming reasonably proficient in constructing sentences requiring subjunctive moods and conditional clauses, and so on, without ever realising that this is a language in which ordinary people quarrel furiously, or make love. The first method may be dangerous, because the people from whom one learns the language may be using it ungrammatically, talking slang, or speaking in a brogue which is not acceptable in educated circles, but at least it has the advantage of being a live method. The second method is far more dangerous (because as every countryman knows, it is not much use flogging a dead horse). Common sense dictates that what is needed is a mixture of both methods.

It seems obvious that every teacher of English should apply the same amount of common sense in teaching children the proper use of their own language. Children learn the English of their parents and their environment first and foremost, and will continue to use this sort of language, despite all efforts to overlay it with a veneer of 'correct English', whenever they are completely free from the shackles of conventional school-room education. This means that every class confronts its teacher with about 75 per cent of its members speaking 'the dialect of the tribe', and the other 25 per cent speaking 'good English' naturally. In the past, the general practice has been to attempt to teach the large majority what amounts to a completely new language by means of constant meaningless exercises, and the repetitive and frustrating correction of the worst mistakes in their natural speech.

The exercises were a complete waste of time. I well remember one of the first English lessons I ever took. I had been given a new set of text-books supposedly suitable for the seven-to-nine age range. The first lesson was about subject and predicate. After explanation and examples, the children were given a list of jumbled subjects for which they had to sort out the right predicates from another jumbled list. At the end of an industrious half hour I was in possession of a lot of new facts that had previously been left out of my own education.

> A policeman rises in the east.
> The sun has a large hump.
> Gratitude is a place full of trees.
> A camel wears a helmet.
> A forest means thankfulness.

The result of this method of teaching has generally been to allow the poor children to fall neatly between two stools, never really grasping the niceties of grammar, but being only too much aware of certain things wrong with their native speech. Then instead of a child rushing in and saying excitedly, 'I done what you said and it looks beautiful', he comes in carefully choosing his words and says, 'I have did what you told me and it looks very nice.'

I am reminded of the bright child of seven who listened patiently to her teacher's lesson on singulars and plurals. She was then required to show what she had learned by putting into sentences of her own some of the examples used in the lesson. The teacher was not at all pleased to read the child's first sentence, which was, 'Mice sometimes have a lot of baby mouses'. This example alone should prove how much English teaching in the past has been done the wrong way round. This particular child had no doubt been politely bored by her teacher's lesson on singulars and plurals, though understanding it well enough. The command to write sentences out of her head released her for a moment from the boredom into her own world of thought and feeling, and her memory reaching back-wards for some association with the word 'mice' had reminded her of the family of babies she had seen and thought adorable. The delightful memory had immediately wiped out all thought of the grammatical object of her sentence, and in her instinctive attempt to differentiate between the parent mouse and the babies she used 'mouses'; for which inattention she was punished by having to write out 'The plural of mouse is mice' for fifteen minutes after school. As she was my own sister, I can vouch for the fact that she would never have used 'mouses' instead of 'mice' in normal conversation. Had her use of the word been completely spontaneous, in 'free' writing, her teacher could probably have deduced the reason for its inclusion, and if it were then shown that she did not in fact know the right plural, could have pointed out to her in two minutes the few queer plurals still left in our language, and made a game of being on the look out for them and listing them for future use, without wasting twenty other children's precious time.

I could see quite plainly that one of my tasks was to 'purify the dialect of the tribe' without devitalising the common speech of the children altogether: to keep what was telling and homely and fine in their brand of English, and to strengthen it with the props of correct grammar, punctuation, and spelling, as far as it could be done without covering up the original structure altogether.

It seemed to me that the first objective was to close the gap between spoken and written English. School life had a tradition that talking was what you did out of school, and writing what you did inside. My pupils were at first as loath to talk inside as they would have been to write in the playground, and had no idea that talking and writing and reading bore any relation to each other. The freedom given to them soon loosened their tongues, and we had long since left behind the days when deathly silence reigned as soon as I appeared, either inside or out. Good conversation is an art in itself, and one that I have always thought well worth acquiring. As the children grew more and more used to me and my ways, they talked freely, not only in front of me, but with me and to me. They began to realise that a good discussion was as exciting as any other sort of contest. They had to obey the rules of good conversation, which meant listening while others talked, keeping to the subject under discussion, and saying only those things that they were prepared to back by further argument if necessary. Discussions ranged far and wide over many different subjects, but nearly always came round, in the end, to questions of religion, ethics and morals. They soon realised that there was nothing I was not prepared to talk to them about, although I sometimes had to tell them outright that I did not know the answers, or that such subjects were better left to a private talk between me and the child concerned. On the subject of sex I found them open and free, to the limit of their knowledge, and without any embarrassment at that age. I felt it my duty to make them aware as much as possible of the everyday, homely relationships between the sexes, the naturalness of seeking friends among the opposite sex, the finding of yin for one's own yan to make a perfect whole in all other ways besides the biological one. In these discussions some parents were a help, but some regarded me with a very wary eye, because a village is always a stronghold of puritanism—on the surface—and old ideas about what children should know die hard. I had two little girls of eight and nine in my class who were showing a great interest in a certain Asian lady who had been staying nearby, and who had, to the eyes of the village, been flaunting her very obvious pregnancy in a most unseemly way by wearing a bright scarlet sari wrapped rather tightly around her. The mother of the two stopped me one day outside the school.

'I don't know what to tell my two', she said earnestly. 'They keep on asking me what makes that woman such a funny shape.'

'Tell them the truth', said I.

Horror at the thought of such indecency spread over her rosy face. 'That I shan't', she said. 'They ain't a-going to know such things yet.'

'Let me tell them, if you would rather not', I volunteered.

She showed indignation in every nerve. 'It ain't your job to tell my child'en such things', she declared.

I bowed to her decision, of course: but I pursued the subject out of amusement and curiosity.

'If you are not going to tell them, and you won't let me,' I said, 'how are they going to find out?'

'They'll find out soon enough', she said. 'Let 'em find out the same way as I did.' I felt this last remark on her part a little unwise, since she had had an illegitimate child at eighteen. Still I persisted. 'Will you tell me what answer you did give them when they asked you the direct question about what was the matter with the lady?' I said.

She replied, rather pleased at her own cleverness at escaping the awkward situation so neatly, I felt, 'Oh, as long as it were her they were asking about, I said, "There's nothing the matter with her. They are like that in India".'

I had to go away and laugh, for the very truth of her remark, bringing a momentary vision of India's teeming millions, seemed to cap the conversation, and I felt that any further word would be an anti-climax.

The children were far more interested in religion than sex. It seemed that they felt an instinctive need for some kind of belief against which to measure their experience of growing up, and they were by no means prepared to accept the orthodox brands of village religion handed out to them at their various Sunday

Schools. They proved beyond any shadow of doubt their capacity to think for themselves.

'Do you believe in hell?' asked a ten-year-old boy.

'Yes, I think so. If you believe in heaven, you must surely believe in hell, too, though I don't know what sort of a place I mean by hell at all.'

'I don't believe there is a hell.'

'Why not?'

'Jesus said that if anybody was sorry for what they had done, God would forgive them. Judas was so sorry for what he had done that he went out and hanged himself, so he would be forgiven. If he is forgiven, surely he must be in heaven. And if men like him are in heaven, whoever can there be left to be in hell?'

Or, on Ascension Day: 'The disciples saw Jesus go up in a cloud, but the two angels said that he would return "in like manner as ye have seen him go". Does that mean that he will come again one day, just dropping out of a cloud?'

Second child: 'Don't be silly. That would mean he would have to come through space to get here, and that isn't possible.'

First child: 'Why not? He could do all sorts of impossible things.'

Second child: 'If he came back in his body, it would wear away and burn out travelling through space, like Professor Chapman said the little Russian dog in the sputnik did that time when we wrote to him.'

Of course it does not really need saying that the importance of such talks was never the conclusions reached, if any, but the value of being able to think, willing to think, and not afraid to put one's thoughts into words. Nevertheless, it was always interesting to me to see how their minds worked, and I have been very sympathetic as well as amused at watching other adults, not so used to children as I, struggling to keep up with the speed at which their thoughts race ahead; it often seemed to me that the child, untrammelled by any experience of what he thought *ought* to be considered, leapt forward into the realm of the purely abstract in a way that left the most studious grown-up theologian standing. On the other hand, there were occasions when the opposite took place, and it was just as illuminating to watch the child struggling to keep up with the adult, trying desperately to follow the adult's instruction on some abstract theme, and falling back on a bit of his own concrete experience to fill the gaps when his understanding failed. I cannot resist one example. A friend of mine, a head teacher at a small village school, had been telling her children about the guardian angels and, on her own confession, had been laying it on a bit thick.

'Wherever you are,' she had said, 'you need never be afraid. In the dark, just as in the daylight, when mummy's there, or when she's not, your angel is always there, looking after you.'

It so happened that down in front of her there sat a little boy who lived at a very outlying and lonely farm called Alicky Farm. When she stopped, he said, wonderingly, 'Are we got angels down at Alicky, then?'

The teacher thought that here she saw a good chance of pushing home the point of her lesson.

'Yes,' she said, 'even down at Alicky, if you are all alone and even in the dark, you needn't be afraid, because you have an angel there, always looking after you.'

The child waited patiently and politely till she had finished, and then dropped his innocent bombshell.

'Well,' he said, 'I reckon that ol' angel's a-wasting his time, 'cos we don't need him. You see, *we're got a good dog.*'

During conversations with my own children, which often began quite spontaneously in the middle of other subjects, I applied the theory which I followed generally in the teaching of English. It was based on the simple formula that if you stand out in the rain long enough, you are bound to get wet, and may even get soaked to the skin. I exposed my children to showers of English used for its true purpose. That the showers they were out in were not absolutely pure English, I had to accept, trying where I could to show the impurities. I never corrected grammar if by doing so I should have interrupted thought, for I consider that to be by far the more important. I drew attention to incidental faults when I could do it without disrupting the conversation, and always made a point of commenting favourably when anyone used a dialect phrase which was self-explanatory and vivid. I allowed them to know how it delighted me to hear the speech of the few people in the village who still used a good old East Anglian brogue, like the farmer-manager who had helped us with the lake village model. I treated them, just for fun, to an occasional spate of the fenland dialect which was my own particular heritage, telling them how proud I was still to have at my command words which my fenland Celtic ancestors might well have been using when the Romans were showing them how to build dykes to drain their fields; and I suggested that such words as they used naturally (when not suppressed altogether by socially ambitious mothers) had probably been used just as excitedly when

> Thorkill and Thurstan from Jutland came
> To harry our homesteads with sword and flame.

As much of the beauty of rural speech is founded on natural imagery, I drew attention to the similarity between the colloquialisms so common to us and the kind of imagery used by the poets; in this way a remark made, for instance, on an occasion when all the rest of the school were clustering round the one holding an injured blackbird:

Don't ruttle round him so, do his poor little heart'll beat faster than ever, an' its gooing like bees' wings now.

135

passed not only uncorrected, but complimented for its apt simile.

My own use of the word simile reminds me to say in passing that in talking to the children I always used the correct terms for the parts of speech, and discussed similes, metaphors, etc., under their proper names from the beginning—a training that stood us all in good stead when, one term, we got caught up in a passion for *The Canterbury Tales*.

So much for spoken English. Good speech depends on a knowledge of words and how to use them, and so does written English. Both, however, are without purpose if there is nothing to be said or written. I wanted to build up in the children a love of English, not merely a knowledge of it. I wanted it to be to them a means whereby they could live their lives and order their experiences more consciously, and to the full. To be able to think clearly is the first thing needed towards 'good English'; to be critically and appreciatively aware of one's own immediate environment is to provide oneself with a criterion against which to judge the tiny, everyday incidents which together make up everybody's experience of life; to comprehend the printed word is to be able to explore the experience of others, farther afield in age, time, and physical distance; and to be able at last to record in words one's own deepest feelings, one's own excursions into the realms of thought and imagination, is to possess the key to the door of mankind's total experience, behind which lies the comprehension of the whole world of art.

I saw my task of teaching English as one complete whole, and as such I continued to teach it. Infants must, of course, be taught to read, and the manual skill of calligraphy. These skills are not ends in themselves. Good handwriting is an asset and an art which can give pleasure, but a beautifully written page saying nothing is a complete waste of time; reading is a wonderful skill to possess, and comprehension greater still, but what is read and its bearing on life is the important thing.

I have no intention of dealing with the mechanics of teaching young children to read, except to offer one word of warning to inexperienced head teachers ordering sets of readers for their infant classes for the first time. That bit of advice is that they should never forget that any new, bright, up-to-the-minute, gaily illustrated, *à-la-mode* expensive reading scheme is mere trash and quite valueless unless the actual English used, however limited the vocabulary, is intrinsically good and *natural*. The same applies, of course, to any book offered to the children at any stage in their education.

Infants learn by imitation and are quick to do so. They must be fed in the earliest stages with nothing but the best, and plenty of it. Their daily meat must be folk-tales and stories, nursery rhymes and jingles, songs and endless conversation. Small children love repetition, and the same good story like 'The Hobyahs' for instance, is better for being told over and over again, till the children can join in with 'Pull down the hemp stalks', and infinitely preferable to a new 'pretty-pretty' story every day.

I happen to like italic writing, and teach it from the very earliest stage, so that by the time the children are six they have at their command a flowing, legible hand, which a little daily practice keeps in trim. There is now no shortage of books for instruction and copy in the italic hand, all of them quite good. The use of pattern making as a preparation for this style has been questioned, but I think it is just as valid for italic writing as for any other. Large, square-ended felt pens, large lettering pens, carpenters' pencils and conté chalks can all be used to give practice and pleasure in the use of a square-ended tool, and this is the first real step to a good italic hand. My children delighted in making patterns with coloured inks and lettering pens, and used these patterns in their own right as decoration and illumination round the pages of the illustrated psalm-books mentioned later on. A favourite way of producing patterns was to lay wax crayon thickly on to shiny paper, then to put a second layer of another colour thickly over the top of the first; the pattern was then made by scratching off the top layer with a sharp tool, leaving the first colour showing through. With italic writing in mind, I provided a set of small screwdrivers for the scratching off process. The sharp, square end of the screwdriver produces exactly the same effect as an italic nib held correctly, and the children's skill in making their patterns 'look like a bit of tape' grew apace. The screwdrivers were in such demand that I had to draw up a rota for the use of the biggest one. One morning it fell to the turn of the most stupid child in the school, an immature, spoilt only child. He took the screwdriver and retired to his desk, and everyone else soon became too engrossed in his own work to notice what the boy was doing with the screwdriver. Then all at once we jumped at the sound of a heavy clatter, as part of the child's desk fell on to the floor. He had used the screwdriver for its proper function, and quietly and systematically unscrewed the screws that held his desk together. The rest of the children were infinitely more shocked than I was and regarded the culprit with inconceivable scorn. Then John, a slow-moving, humorous, delightful boy with a pronounced speech impediment looked at him witheringly, back at me significantly, and said, touching his own temples, 'He might have done better if he had used it on himself, up here'. Then without another word, John put down the book he was reading, and stepping gingerly among paint and paper spread all over the floor, removed the screwdriver from the abashed child's hand and proceeded to put the desk together again. I find such small incidents unforgettable, however many years pass. They were part and parcel of the whole experiment of running a school as a single unit, complete in itself but made up of free individuals cemented together by common interests, mutual trust, mutual respect, and love.

To return to the question of writing practice: pattern making should be interspersed with practice in making the letter shapes, and the best guide for these is the shape the teacher is going to use himself, because this is the one the children will see on the blackboard and everywhere else the teacher sets his hand. If, therefore, the teacher can do without the copy-books from the beginning, he will find his task easier as the time goes on; but if the teacher is unsure of his own hand, it is much better to allow the children to copy from really good examples than his own half-formed style. Handwriting is an art, after all, and should be taught as such. There is no virtue in using any one particular style unless that style can be brought as near to perfection as small hands can execute. Daily practice in the art of writing is essential, and the time spent in doing it need by no means be wasted, even with children whose hand is already well formed. It is quite easy to make double use of this time, if the passages for copying are selected with care and an eye on the language.

To achieve the few minutes' practice every day with the minimum of fuss, I made dozens of writing copy-cards, choosing for them all the age-old, well-worn rhymes, jingles, weather sayings and so on that are so dear to the hearts of children and country people especially. They could not read the rhymes when they began to copy them, but they knew I could, and brought the card of their choice to me to be read. Then when the writing was finished they had the pleasure of drawing a picture to go with it. In this way, word, thought and interpretation went along together from the very beginning, under the disguise of learning to write.

> Lock the dairy door! Lock the dairy door!
> Chickle-chackle-chee! I haven't got the key!

There is no rural child but would recognise this, read as it should be, as the language of cocks and hens, and the pictures at the end of the morning's writing practice would be sparkling with life and keen observation and feeling, which a straight-forward suggestion to draw 'hens in the yard' would never produce at that age.

Once a day, the word–thought–picture process was reversed. The children brought out 'the books-we-are-making' (their term) and wrote the next bit of the story that they happened to have on hand. This writing of their own stories was started from the very first, too, long before the children could read. This time the thought came from them, and was interpreted by means of a picture. When the picture was finished, each one told me what it was about, and I wrote for them a few words about their picture. Most of the stories were of the self-projection type, and nearly all the sentences read 'John lives on a farm. He has a big tractor' or 'Philip has a new bike. He can ride to see his Nanna.' I found this a great aid to learning to read, not only because the children understood straight away what the use of words was, but by reading back the story to themselves by means of their own pictures, they trained their memory for the accompanying words.

This writing-reading, reading-writing, treated always as one subject, produced some interesting results. I have kept a set of books all by one child, between the ages of four and a half and seven years, which make a most valuable study of infant progress.

Jeffrey came to me at four, a bright little fellow with a mop of wonderful auburn curls and a gift of romancing which one morning caused him to rush into school declaring that a sow had just bitten his head off 'down by the church'. He showed skill in handling crayons and writing tools straight away, so I made him a sewn book and began on an illustrated version of 'The

House that Jack Built', a rhyme which he knew. He drew all the pictures, and after each one copied, in his fashion, the appropriate text. Next came a book called 'The Farmer', in which he himself thought up a situation every day and drew a picture of it; then I came along, wrote for him what he wanted to say, and he copied it. As soon as this was finished he demanded a new book in which to write the 'story of my donkey—the one that ran away'. As he had never had a donkey, I recognised his romantic imagination at work, and was delighted at the thought of it being put to such good use. This book was full of the most wonderful, lively pictures and it was evident that Jeff was often considerably irked by the necessity of having to wait for me to write down for him what he wanted to say. He was by this time only a month or two over five years old, but was already beginning to read and I used to find him struggling valiantly on bits of odd paper to write for himself the next part of the tale.

Then we reached the long summer holiday. After it, Jeff returned to me a much more mature little boy, and though still only five and a half, was reading very well when we had been a month or so into the new term. His new book was called 'Jeff the Brave Cowboy', and this time he wrote for himself on a piece of paper. I corrected it, and the fair copy was made into his book. This book was really remarkable for the sudden leap forward he made in his use of English. It was vigorous and economical, with adjectives and adverbs appearing quite naturally in the right places, but only where they were needed for extra emphasis.

One day Jeff was riding over the mountains some Indians shot at Jeff the brave cowboy.

[Next page upside down in the excitement]

Jeff hid beInd a big rock. He waited till the Indians got near him. Then Jeff drew his gun and waited till the Indians got near.

141

Jeff drew his six-shooter. Bang bang bang it went and shot the Indians.

They fell on to the ground.

The undoubted success of 'The Brave Cowboy' put Jeff's feet firmly on the road to authorship. He was away on 'The Dog Fight' before the previous one was really finished, because, having seen a dog fight on his way to school one morning, he simply could not wait to start putting down his memory of it. This was a change from the purely imaginative work of his previous creations and very good as English practice, for he discovered not only the value of possessing powers of keen observation, but of knowing the language that allowed one to record what one had noticed in detail.

It appeared that Jeff's mother, a glorious red-head like himself, had thrown a bucket of water over the fighting dogs. While he was drawing the picture of this, giving his mother unmistakable hair, he was thinking deeply about it, for he must have been wondering how to record the *mood* of the moment in words. He came to me for advice. Although he was still only five years old, I explained to him the use of conversation marks, thinking that that was what he had asked. He was not satisfied.

'Does that make it say *how* Mummy said it?' he asked. 'She didn't just say "Stop it". She said [miming the throwing of the water and stamping his foot] "STOP IT!"'

After Christmas Jeff, now six, wanted to write a pirate story. After reading some pirate books, he started on 'Jeff and the Flying Bird', this time writing straight into his own book without any correction or other interference from me.

One day [Jeff] stood on the prow off his ship. he lookted in his telscope.
What did he see?
He saw a ship sailing across the sea to Jeffs ship.
Attack shouted Jeff.

At seven he wrote 'Jeff the Space Man', text in pencil but pictures in coloured inks. At the end of his first session with his new book, he came to me to show it. I was sitting at my desk, he standing by the side of it. I took the book from him, admired the picture, and read aloud:

Jeff pulled the lever and pressed the button. The space ship swished up into the air and was gone—.

I happened to glance at the real Jeff, who was pressing with all his might an imaginary button on the side of my desk, after which he held the pit of his stomach and gazed at the school ceiling.

'Gosh', he said, in an awed voice, 'can't you just hear it?' I could. 'The ssspace ssship sssswisssshed—.' Of course! After that Jeff went on exercising his imagination, his observation, and his increasing command of English, in book after book after book. His last was a treatise on freshwater fish and how to catch them. At eleven-plus his I.Q. showed him to be only of good average intelligence. I mention this just to prove that he was not the brilliantly academic type of child from whom one would expect this lively interest in English as a matter of course.

Before giving more examples of this free writing of books, I want to make quite clear two essential facts about them as I use them. These books are always profusely illustrated, the picture always being drawn *before the appropriate text is written*. Thought must precede written work, and the picture first serves to inspire and then order thought, so that the words flow with confidence and clarity afterwards. The practice of illustrating a poem or story after it has once been written, pleasant though it may be, has no such value, and if the words have been satisfying enough in their own right, the very sensitive child may even be irked by being asked to do the same thing twice. If the picture is always done first, one finds that the illustrations get fewer and fewer as the children gain more and more confidence in the use of words, finally disappearing except for those put in for sheer pleasure and the delight of making a good thing even better.

The second point is that once the children have acquired enough skill in writing English to write directly into their books with pencil, these books are not corrected, in the ordinary sense of that word. Their authors know that they may write what they please as long as it is legible and comprehensible. This does not mean that they are not read and appreciated. My usual practice is to take each child alone, with his book, reading it all as it progresses, and 'correcting' a page here and there, by which I mean that I point out mistakes and allow them to be rubbed out and the correction made by the owner. In this way the pages remain entirely the child's own, unspoilt by red markings. If the explanation of the nature of the mistakes has been given well enough, the author may then retire with the eraser and proceed to correct the rest of his work himself, thereby learning more than gallons of red ink would have taught him.

As this kind of generative English goes largely 'uncorrected', and as I have a settled hate of unproductive English exercise 'drill', I felt a need for a little 'formal' English to go on alongside the really 'free' work. All my children had a 'composition' book, wherein they offered, once or twice a week, a piece of English to be marked carefully, and judged objectively, credit being given for content, style, grammar and punctuation; and for which we had a system of star awards. In awarding the stars I did not judge alone; I marked carefully and gave the star for everything but the actual content. Then the compositions were all read aloud by their authors, and criticism offered by the other children, who then voted for each and another star was given for the content. It was a matter of surprise to me always to notice how keen, able and just this criticism was, and if, at the end of the lesson, we had a ceremony of presenting a gold star, the applause at the end was spontaneous and sincere. Here are two poems granted gold stars in this way:

The Weeping Willow

I walked across to the willow tree;
Sadly, weeping, it hung its branches of beauty,
Sobbing, 'What poor creature but I
Has to stand in the trickling water?'
It sadly asked.
The river proudly demanded,
'What ungrateful creature but you
Would ask such simple question?
The poplar stands by me,
And enjoys my rushing cloak'.
The willow sobbed and turned away,
Tears running down its branches.
And all I said was,
'Be thankful you are here'.   (BEVERLY, 10.)

Bonfire Night

Whizz! Up went a rocket,
Leaving the ground behind.
The jumping crackers, the bangers,
Are banging at the same time.
Then 'CRACK' goes the bonfire,
Down come the logs.

Round and round
Go the Catherine wheels,
And suddenly stop.
Down falls the guy
From his high
Chair. His head falls off,
And down it goes,
Into the roaring flames.
Soon they will all go out.
Then there is not
One more single sound to be heard.   (ANGELO, 10.)

To return to the story books once more, and to prove the point I made about the value of the picture as thought-promoter when used before the text, I must quote Sarah, a brilliant child who at five wrote her own autobiography, on the last page of which I read 'Now I am nearly six, and that is THE END'.

At six, using ink, Sarah wrote an imaginary tale called 'Jane and the Friendly Bear', which told the story of a small girl, who, lost in the forest, was taken care of by a bear. Sarah brought out her morning's work for me to inspect—a page of writing and a rather mediocre picture executed in ink. It showed the bear's house in the forest. I took a quick glance at it, and being very much occupied with another child, said, 'You have forgotten the chimneys, Sarah.' She did not reply, but went away, and after a few minutes brought her book up again and left it on my desk. At the foot of the page she had added: 'The reason why the bear's house has no chimneys is because bears have such thick warm coats they don't need fires'.

As the children progress up the school, these books become more than a means of gaining confidence and skill and getting English to flow. They begin to serve a much deeper and more fundamental purpose, that of satisfying the need for ordering thought about life as they experience it, giving, as they do, a link between the tangible world and the intangibles of imagination, phantasy, desire and despair. So it was that Jeff's last book might be a treatise on freshwater fish, in the disguise of an imaginary 'Fishing Holiday'; Sarah's 'Adventure at Little Gidding', a self-projection backwards into history, sparked off by a visit to the place and my incidental quotation of

> It would be the same at the end of the journey
> If you came at night like a broken king

which had just enough of mystery in it to set Sarah wanting to know every detail of this poignant moment of history, and finally to inspire her imagination to give herself a part in the drama of it. Angelo will have been carried away once again by his delight in line-drawing, and his delicate fairy story will be wrapped around some minute detail which will give full scope to his visual perception and imagination. Jill will be writing yet another adventure on the farm she hopes to work on in due course, while another, already a little disturbed by thoughts of love and marriage, writes a forward self-projection of a different kind. I take the passage from 'Betty meets her Boy friend'.

One night I said I was going to a dance so I got ready to go. I put my best dress on and went to the door, then down the street I went. All the lights were on round the hall. At the dance a man said Will you dance. I said Yes and we danced all night till twelve o'clock and then he took me home in his car and when we was on the main road he put his arm round me and kissed me.

On the next page they went for a walk in the woods.

Ralph picked one flower. We was so hot we sat on the ground. He kissed me again and made me go all red

(When they got home, Mum said 'What? Another boy friend?')

This is no sniggering, giggling adolescent with a guilty secret; it is the work of a little girl going forward with confidence and sincerity, with understanding and acceptance, and above all, with hope to the next and perhaps best stage of her life. I cannot help feeling that there is hope that adolescence will prove less painful and more the joy it ought to be for this girl because she has taken this chance to meet it on such friendly terms before any kind of guilt has crept in to spoil the acquaintance.

Lastly, there was Beverly, the born creative artist; beautiful, difficult, full of passion and sensibility, living always in two worlds at the same time; the real world, incomprehensible and unsympathetic, but which for Beverly had a magic casement through which she could escape to another world all her own.

Whatever Beverly touched, she turned to art. Her performance as Mary in our Christmas Nativity play would have wrung tears from a clod; paint and clay in her hands took on life of their own; conversation with her sent one away uplifted by her penetrating understanding and flashes of wit; but the written word was her greatest gift, as the limitation of her sense of number was to prove a hindrance to her.

In her books, right from the beginning, Beverly employed phantasy as her medium, exploring always the distant and the unknown; using an element of magic to make all things possible, she was able to live out in her stories the situations of her dreams. Her passion for animals, cats in particular, led her into jungles and zoological gardens, in stories of the 'Puss in Boots' variety in her actual infancy; but by the time she had passed her eighth birthday she had need to project herself still further. Then one day she hit upon an idea so brilliant that thereafter her pen flowed unceasingly as she unravelled skein after skein of her imaginary existence. She simply identified herself with a black cat called Wendy, who had the most astounding adventures, unbounded by space or time. I quote the spontaneous beginning of the series of stories which afterwards delighted us all.

Wendy goes to the Moon

Wendy is a big black cat. One day she saw a see-saw. She was a very bad cat, so she got on one end of it. No sooner had she done this, than a foot-ball bounced on the other end of it and up she went! But—she did not come down again! Instead, she was soaring up, up, up, into the sky. Night came, she was in stratosphere, and in a few minutes more she was in ionosphere.

'OH!' she gasped, for she was a few yards now from the MOON!

Beverly's vivid, intense imagination, coupled with her extraordinary command over language, made her work quite outstanding, though perhaps the continual substitution of this imaginary world for the real one was also unusual. Wendy had adventures so many and various that I can only leave the titles to speak for themselves.

Wendy goes to Sea.	Wendy goes to Hell.
Wendy goes to Fairyland.	Wendy goes into the Past.
Wendy goes to the Circus.	Wendy goes into the Future.
Wendy goes to Heaven.	Wendy meets her Sweetheart.

Wendy goes on her Honeymoon.

I was quite startled to read the last, for it took me back in a flash more than thirty years to another cat-human family. Wendy and Professor Mouser-Thom-Catt (a lecturer at Cambridge, where he had rescued Wendy from a nasty wetting when her punt pole stuck along the Backs) went (like my own)—to YARMOUTH for their honeymoon!

So much for the work that was freer than just 'free'. There still remained the mountain of work that was done freely, that is, spontaneously, happily, willingly and still individually, though under a light but firm control. We were so used to paint that we longed for new effects. We found them with the paper mosaic. In brief, this consists of cutting up glossy-magazine coloured illustrations into tiny, roughly square pieces, and using them as the stones are used in a mosaic. The bare outlines of the picture to be done are executed very sketchily in chalk, and the paste is used as the plaster in a fresco, a piece of the background paper being pasted and the small piece applied rapidly before the paste dries. This process seems to satisfy something in every child. There is the cutting, the sticking, the selecting, and the joy of seeing the picture grow in the infinite range of tones available. The proof of this pudding is in the eating, for the results were of such brilliance that they made our painted pictures, for all their glory, look moonlit in comparison. They taught the children more about colour and texture than years of paint alone could have done.

In our new medium we followed and illustrated the lives of

some of the more popular saints. The choice of subject was a happy one, for the results had all the naïve brilliance of medieval art, and the pictures were conceived with the same child-like innocence and lack of imposed sophistication that characterises the early medieval wall-paintings like those, for instance, in our own parish church.

I know that a great deal of criticism has been offered by all sorts of people about the making of paper mosaics, and I feel bound to answer some of the more obvious doubts about them. One of the commonest complaints is that they take far too long, and that the children get tired of them long before they can finish them. This may be true, particularly with young children, but in general this criticism does not apply if the organisation is good and if the teacher is not finicky about it. The picture must be conceived in big, bold outlines. Then the artist decides which bit he will start on, finds paper the colour he wants and cuts it very quickly into approximate squares. When he has prepared his small pieces of colour, he pastes the background and applies the small pieces very quickly, over-lapping them so as to make a solid mass of colour. When the whole picture has been covered, the result may appear very indistinct and blurred, but in a mosaic a black outline is perfectly legitimate, and it will be found that this outline, which can be done in paint with a fairly small brush, will pull the picture out.

Of course, if any teacher insists on the small tiles being cut in exact squares with a ruler and set-square, and then laid side by side with precision, or cut to fit curves, and so on, the process ceases to be art and becomes technique, and takes so long that any junior child would be fed up with it long before he had any results to show. I have seen most beautiful things done this way by one of my colleagues in a secondary modern school, where the aim was not so much to create a picture using paper instead of paint, as to teach what a real mosaic was, and to emphasise the part played by the light falling on the tiny separated squares of paper. In the junior school I very seldom encouraged the smaller children to undertake a mosaic alone, though often they insisted. This kind of work can be done so well by children working in a team that it seems a pity not to use the valuable social training it offers. One child finds the colours, one cuts, one sticks. If, however, a small child fired with ambition undertakes a task too large for him to finish, and shows signs of being weary of it, the answer is not to waste the effort that has already been put into it in the first flush of enthusiasm, but to allow him to finish it very quickly with paint or crayon or both. The mixture is quite often the most exciting thing about it.

Many teachers have been put off, too, by the mosaics they have seen which have been done in the dreadful, garish coloured papers supplied commercially for what used to be called 'paper work' with infants. This paper usually has a gummed surface, and the trains, windmills, and so on I have seen done in junior schools with the horrible stuff have been enough to turn my stomach. The best colour of all is that provided by the coloured illustrations of the ubiquitous 'women's' magazines, the glossier the better. These will come from home in large quantities on request, and cost nothing. Any paperhanger's paste will do to stick it on with, though the new ones which do not leave smears on the surface are undoubtedly the best.

It does seem necessary to say once more that my way is not necessarily the only way, nor perhaps the best. Everybody who tries my ideas out will arrive at a quite different result, and so they should. By experimenting boldly enough they may discover an altogether new process. One need not, for instance, stick to small pieces of paper. One of my greatest treasures is an enormous work, about ten feet square, of the Nativity of Christ. The figures in it are three-quarters life size, and the whole is done to represent a stained glass window. The coloured illustrations of magazines were used as before, but each piece was cut out as large as it could be. Then the figure of Joseph was composed of all the pieces of green put together, Mary of the blues, and so on. The greens varied in shade like every other colour, and it was soon discovered what wonderful use the variations of tone could be put to. Then each piece of colour was strapped round with black insulation tape to represent the lead of a window. For a small and delicate work, coloured tissue papers set behind cut-out outlines of black or white tougher paper give a marvellous effect, especially if mounted where the light can fall through them.

The mention of our stained glass nativity picture reminds me that of course there is no need to stick to paper for making such pictures. Material such as cloth is even better, because one has the added joy of the different textures to play with. The cutting to shape and size of material for pictures is the most valuable practice for needlework I can think of, into the bargain. Again, may I offer a word of advice and warning? Though the materials used need not cost anything, and can be brought from home as a rule, it is a mistake to imagine that beautiful things will somehow appear miraculously out of a dirty old rag-bag. If the interesting pieces of stuff are crumpled or dirty, they must be washed and ironed and folded carefully away, so as to be ready and pleasant to use. Another set of boxes can contain oddments of fur, leather, feathers, braid, and so on.

Mention of Christmas also brings to mind the delights of preparing in other ways for this happy season in school. To the class at home with art materials, the possibilities are endless, and I do not propose even to start on making suggestions for decorations, except to say that I do hope that by 'decoration' it is understood that I do not mean paper-chains. I will mention some of the many, many different ways my children and I have in the past celebrated the origin of Christmas in school. First, we always made Christmas books, year after year. In them, we simply told the story of the birth of Jesus in our own words, illustrating as we went along. Every child from four to eleven had the same sort of home-made book to start on, though the older children had more pages in theirs. The tiny children had pictures only, with a caption here and there written by me or by an older child, or perhaps a line from a well-known carol. The older infants began to write in a few sentences with each picture, the younger juniors included the words of carols they were learning (and often the music, too), and illustrated profusely in anything they could lay their hands on; and at the top of the school, competition ran high to see who could produce the most original ideas. One book I still have contains the Christmas story most beautifully and simply written, and every illustration is conceived and executed as a 'pop-up' scene; another contains a whole series of new carols written by the child herself; another is filled with Christmas customs in other countries. Meanwhile, we all joined in a co-operative Christmas frieze, depicting the events of the first Christmas, to fit our large display boards all round the schoolroom. Then there was the crib, which we supplied for our lovely little church for several years. We made cribs of as many different things as we made pictures. We made them in clay, unfired but painted; fired, and afterwards painted; slip-decorated and fired; in separate figures, put together on a base of an infant table covered with straw, and overhung with a canopy of blue cloth over a hoop held up by split canes, and from which crêpe paper angels with silver wings, hung on invisible black thread, fluttered in the slightest breeze. We made the figures one year of solid papier mâché, each figure being made firm and solid by the simple device of moulding the papier mâché round a bottle, and leaving the bottle inside. Kneeling figures were made in

153

exactly the same way on tiny bottles, and heads were made to bend by being constructed separately around a tube of cardboard, which was inserted into the neck of the bottle and fastened at the required angle with Sellotape before the wet papier mâché was put round the neck. The following year we made the bottles hold our figures again, but this time we used a different technique. We constructed head and hands from papier mâché as we might have done for marionettes. The head we inserted into a bottle or a cardboard tube, and fixed pipe-cleaner wire round to support the arms. Then we dipped lengths of material—the best was very cheap, coarse but stiff cotton crash—into a fairly thick mixture of plaster of Paris and, while the plaster was still wet, draped the cloth round the bottle or tube, making folds where they fell naturally, and tying the little figures round at waist and wrist, or wherever we wanted to shape the cloth. When the plaster had set, the figures were white and stiff. Handling them to colour them afterwards was a delicate job, because the plaster tended to flake off, but as they were standing firmly, the actual amount of handling was small, and the plaster took the colour (I used a temperapaste) excellently. The finished crib was one of the best we ever made. The figures were a good deal larger than anything we had ever been able to accomplish before, and much more colourful. The angels made by the same method were much too heavy to be suspended by cotton, so we had to think up another setting. This time we used an old clothes horse, covered with an old curtain dyed midnight blue. The angels stood away from it, supported by black covered wire, such as florists use. The stable was made of logs brought by the children, and thatched with dried Michaelmas daisy stalks; a living Christmas tree about 3 feet high stood behind it, and from the top of the tree an invisible wire held a tiny electric star. Another tiny bulb hung in a lantern at the back of the stable, and no more light was needed. The whole effect was strangely medieval, and seemed to ask for even more brilliance of colour. We set it up in the corner of the church against the white wall, and the colour it seemed to need was red. A red linen tablecloth, red curtains, and a red bedspread appeared, and we draped the tables the crib stood on, as well as two larger clothes horses than the one that held the sky, to flank the whole scene on both sides. The effect was breathtaking.

For sheer power to stir the heart I would still choose the last crib we ever made. In this one we limited the number of figures to the Holy Family, and three shepherds. The children were split into five groups, and each group undertook to make one figure. The idea was that the figures should be life-sized, made exactly to the measurements of one of the children in the group. Much measuring and recording of statistics went on. The method by which we hoped to accomplish this was by the very easy method of building up the required shape with crumpled newspaper dipped in 'Polycell'. We found that we had to have some support for the standing figures, and after much experiment discovered that rolled newspapers were by far the best. Skeletons of rolled newspapers were constructed, on which the soaked newspapers were built up. Unfortunately, I had forgotten that this material always shrinks considerably in drying, so although our figures remained very nicely in proportion, they were only about two-thirds of the size we had intended. When dry, their faces were painted, and they were given stuck-on hair. They were then dressed, with cloth cut out and sewn, stuck, pinned or otherwise secured by the children into the design they had in mind. The group was then set up on the floor, which had been littered with straw, and a shelter was arranged from the clothes-horses, this time covered with sacking. The sacking in turn was draped with long trails of dark green, glossy ivy leaves, matted and tangled together. The crude simplicity with which the whole had been achieved

155

gave the figures such humble dignity and such an air of reality that it was overwhelming.

Something of the same nature might be said, I think, about the many Nativity plays that we put on, either in the church or in the school itself. They bore very little relation to what is usually meant by 'drama' in primary schools; they included everybody, good, bad and indifferent: we had no special lighting effects, no proper costumes, above all no scripted play. We hung the same well-known and beloved story on a different peg each year, and having once got the theme into our heads, tried out ideas until the best bits began to fit together to make a whole. We only wrote the script down at the last minute, when practice had given it some permanence, but even then it was always open to a bit of spontaneous dialogue, as on the never-to-be-forgotten occasion when the only girl in the school with complete inability to sound the letter 'h' was playing the inn-keeper's wife. She was an excellent little actress, and put her heart and soul into the performance. When her errant husband, played by Jeffrey of the red head, made his appearance, she had a speech in which she rated him for being late when she had so much to do with the inrush of visitors to Bethlehem. 'Where have you been?' she asked, as practised. 'I've been so busy I didn't know which way to turn' and then, impromptu and quite out of the blue, she added, throwing out her arms and jerking her head to indicate the inn behind her 'This 'hole 'ouse is 'umming like a bee-'ive!' These plays achieved the same quality of naturalness combined with deep feeling and self-assurance on the part of the children as the best of the art work and the best of the poetry, and the crib described above; I do not know if experts would have called them 'drama', but I have no hesitation at all in calling them 'art'.

I had always used the Bible as a source for the inspiration of pictorial art as well as for its more usual purpose. We had, from the beginning, drawn or painted pictures of stories we had read and discussed in the R.E. lesson, whether it was the whale disgorging Jonah (though in actual fact we found the expression of this dramatic story in 'modern movement'), or the Transfiguration. Moses coming down the mountain with a tablet under each arm inspired Derek to a crayon masterpiece, while Philip's 'Peter walking on the Water', painted with a limited palette of black, blue, white and yellow had an other-worldliness that was eerie. Sometimes it was just the words that prompted the picture, as with Beverly's 'And a little child shall lead them', and occasionally the other way round, as on the morning when the whole class had been told to draw the Israelites crossing the Red Sea, and Sarah's 'picture' had consisted of a piece of *vers libre* on the subject, instead.

> We've had a wretched time in Egypt
> So I'm glad I trusted Moses
> And I hope old Pharoah's sorry
> That he ever kept us for his slaves at all.

It was another happy chance, however, that provided the real link between art and English-cum-Scripture.

I had been brought up a Methodist, and when, at this period of my life, I joined the congregation of the Church of England, I found the inclusion of a chanted psalm in the services a delight, and sang away lustily, after my uninhibited Non-conformist fashion into the deep roof of the church, knowing that my voice would be lost anyway up among the beams and that no one would hear my breathless attempts to follow the 'pointings' in my prayer book. One Sunday we were singing Psalm 104 and I was enjoying it as usual when to a detached section of my consciousness it occurred that what the psalm really was was a series of pictorial images wrapped up in deceptively simple words and parcelled together in unforgettable phrases. In the words of a hymn known to me from childhood, I could see that the kindness shown to me in being able to enjoy a psalm as much as this was not meant for me alone, and that I had to pass it on. I could hardly wait for the next morning to share my discovery with the children. My enthusiasm worked upon them like a charm, and before the term was out we had produced our first pictorial psalm. Each page was an illustration of a complete phrase. Facing it was the text, writ large in coloured ink, and decorated fittingly with a border of patterns.

'The trees of the Lord are full of sap; the cedars of Lebanon,
which he hath planted'

Sometimes the children worried about the meaning. 'He touches the hills and they smoke.' 'What does that mean? Hills don't smoke.'

'Don't they? What about volcanoes?'

Out came the reference books, and interest in volcanoes ran high. The next morning brought a copy of *The Last Days of Pompeii* taken from the film of that name produced many years ago, and complete with lurid 'stills': a series of photographs of Fujiyama taken by an older brother ex-pupil of the school while on National Service, and a stone from the crater of Etna, gathered by an uncle a year or two before. General knowledge was not the least of the by-products of studying a psalm in detail.

On the other hand, quite often the simple, child-like acceptance that the words meant what they said produced pictures at once amusing and disturbing to an adult, as when Jill, then aged about six and a half, read:

The Lord lifteth up the meek: He casteth the wicked down to the ground.

Without question she proceeded to draw an absolutely literal representation of it, which showed God standing firmly with legs well apart, arms raised and palms flat, while on his hands, also with legs wide astride, stood 'the meek', a little girl about Jill's own age, and all around the wicked lay supine, with their useless guns, knives and coshes fallen from their nerveless hands.

'There go the ships' portrayed the *Queen Mary* steaming regally into harbour surrounded by tugs and other small craft, and 'He shall give his angels charge over thee; they shall bear thee up, lest thou dash thy foot against a stone' pictured two hefty angels giving a bowler-hatted business man a leg-up over a lump of rock.

The effect of this language on the children's own English can be imagined. Where else could you get images so vivid, phrases of such cadence, sentences of such simple clarity?

He giveth snow like wool;
He scattereth the hoar frost like ashes:
He casteth forth his ice like morsels:
Who can stand before his cold?

That the psalms were poetry of the highest order was not lost upon these children who through their pictures grew to know and love them. They began to comprehend that poetry had a different function from prose, and that it was another art which for its own sake was worth cultivating. Once they had accepted this premise, they seemed to know instinctively when poetry was a better medium for what they had to say than prose, and vice versa. As their copious free story work gave them ample practice in writing prose, a good deal of their formal work took on poetic form. I encouraged this tendency whenever it was not in any way forced, both because it gave a certain freedom from the convention of 'composition', and also because the form imposed by the poetic structure gave the children greater confidence in using unusual sentence pattern, cadence, pause for effect, and so on. Look carefully at this spontaneous piece of work by Beverly, aged ten: I give it first as prose.

Everything is silent. Even the leaves do not stir in the evening breeze. An owl-hoot sounds through the darkness in the clear cool night. That owl hoot, that warning cry, chills every mouse to the marrow. The owl sees a wandering shape and flies closer to this thing. The unsuspecting mouse sees its vicious attacker and starts to panic. It runs to and fro. With a too-whit, too-whoo the owl swoops down to make the mouse his prisoner. There's a shriek, a cry, then it stops. The owl has slaughtered his helpless captive, and with a flutter of his wing he flies back into the darkness, and silence is restored.

Leaving out the respect one must have for the sensitivity of this piece, I think there are few who will not admit that it is a very good piece of work from an average ten-year-old. Yet I am sure that if I had been marking it as written above, I should have thought that it was perhaps a little too fancy, too flowery, too precious, to have the ring of real sincerity which I want above all else in a child's work. I should have been in difficulty to point this out to Beverly without damaging the delicate antennae of her approach to English. But such was Beverly's sensitivity that she did not offer this to me as I have given it above. I saw it first as given below:

Night Hunter

Everything is silent.
Even the leaves do not stir in the evening breeze.
An owl-hoot sounds through the darkness
In the clear cool night.
That owl hoot,
That warning cry,
Chills every mouse to the marrow.
The owl sees a wandering shape,
It flies closer to this thing.
The unsuspecting mouse sees its vicious attacker,
The frightened mouse starts to panic,
It runs to and fro.
With a too-whit too-whoo the owl swoops down,
To make the mouse his prisoner.
There's a shriek,
A cry,
Then it stops.
He has slaughtered his helpless captive.
With a flutter of his wing
He flies back into the darkness.
Silence is restored.

As prose it is slightly fanciful, a little too dramatic, and over-done, even for a ten-year-old deliberately striving to exploit a knowledge of words. But it was not written as prose: it was conceived, and *felt* as poetry, and as such has considerable merit, in my opinion.

That owl hoot,
That warning cry,
Chills....

The pause at the line break on 'hoot' and 'cry' gives extra significance to two commonplace words, and the short, repeated rhythm has the effect of heightening tension: but the complete success of these two lines is only felt fully in the surprise of the next line,

> Chills every *mouse* to the marrow

when the flesh creeps with the shock of becoming the doomed mouse in the shadow of those silent, threatening wings.

Then there is the controlled lengthening of the line, and the repetition of 'unsuspecting mouse' and 'frightened mouse' as suspense grows, brought again to crystallisation of the futile struggle against the inevitability of death by the ordinariness of

> It runs to and fro.

Lastly, the 'f' sounds of the ending lines

> With a flutter of his wings
> He floats back into the darkness

have exactly the soft sound of owls' wings in the night, a sound without sound. The effect is to leave one with a feeling that the owl itself bears no blame for the death of the mouse: that being a creature of darkness, it has acted only in accordance with its own, mysterious inner light. If this child had written the prose into which I turned her lovely poem, it would have been spurious prose for a child of her age, and therefore poor English. In this context I hesitate to quote anyone as pedagogic as Mr Hugh Kenner, but it just happens that in dealing with Eliot's appropriation of a sermon by Lancelot Andrewes almost word for word for the beginning of the Journey of the Magi, he makes the very point about the difference in feeling between the same thing said as poetry or as prose. (I am not suggesting that Bishop Andrewes' prose needed correcting.) Mr Kenner says, after quoting both Andrewes' prose, and Eliot's poetic adaptation of it,

> It is not the specific borrowing that is noteworthy, *but the mode of organising a sentence so that the lineation will coincide with its very bones.*

It seems to me that as there is something of the artist in every child, there is also something of the poet; for it is precisely this organisation of sentences so that every word tells that children seem to be able to do instinctively. They 'heir it' as my father would have said, in a direct line from Chaucer, through Shakespeare, the psalms, folk-tales and jingles, and last, but by no means least, the forceful, natural image-packed idiom of their forebears. So, once it is established that poetry is as natural as prose but that they both have their separate uses, the children are as free with one as with the other. One of the results of this in my school was that the infants just beginning to write things of their own other than their story-books often produced pages that it would puzzle anyone to name either as poetry or prose, though they usually leaned more to the poetic by reason of significant repetition and cadence, and this though the word 'poetry' had never been used before them of their own work. Irene was seven and a few weeks when she heard me suggest to the middle 'group', that is, the seven-to-nine age group, to which she did not really belong, being technically 'an infant' still, that they should go and stand out in the soft gentle rain for a minute or two and then come in and write down anything they thought about it. She decided to join this expedition, and I quote her 'written work':

> When I saw rain in the village
> Of course that was when I got up from bed
> I got dressed and I said to myself I said
> I am going to go out,
> I am going to see how it feels
> How it feels outside I am going to see
> So I went out under a tree and it was funny
> How it shook the rain down on my head.

I am perfectly well aware what will happen when a great many infant and junior teachers read that. They will say, scornfully,

'If that is what she calls poetry, then all our children do it. This is only the repetitive rubbish children always write when they start written work, and it looks like poetry because instead of putting a full stop at the end and a capital letter at the beginning of a sentence, this child has misunderstood and put a capital letter at the beginning of each new line.'

Just so, precisely. I give them full marks for detecting it. But their knowing that does not alter the real issue in the very least. What Irene wrote was poetry, and there is no denying it, however it was that she came to do it. I issue the challenge then, to just those teachers. When your infants produce bits of work like that, what are you going to do about it? Use it as poetry, and a stepping stone to a work like Beverly's 'Night Hunter' and the appreciation of Shakespeare in due course, or insist on the full stops and capital letters being correctly placed, thereby reducing this lovely felt experience of rain to a dehydrated, desiccated composition about 'A Wet Day' in the time honoured fashion of children?

It is wet to day. The road is wet. The path is wet. The roof is wet. I do not like the wet, etc., etc., etc.

(When I was young, I once set a class of juniors to write about 'The Milkman'. I knew no better, then. One child handed me in a page full of neat writing. I read: 'The milkman brings the milk, milk, milk, milk, milk, milk, milk, milk—' a hundred and fifty-three times. Since then I have often spent part of my summer holiday helping friends who run a large retail dairy to deliver milk. How right that child's perception was! After the two-hundredth bottle or so, one begins to realise that that is all there is to say about the milkman. The fault was not hers, it was mine. Praise be that I know better now, and no longer inflict that kind of torture on my children.)

Irene's kind of work can soon be turned to poetry which is

'at least as well written as prose'. I am going to give a good many examples from all kinds of different children, so that I cannot be accused of recommending something for all children, on the evidence that a few inspired children like Beverly can and will do it well. Before doing that, however, I want to say a word or two more about the poetry children produce.

Sometimes one has the pleasure of reading a poem by a witty, intelligent child who has exploited his command of English with deliberate intent, thereby reaching a point of almost staggering sophistication. Such was Sarah's poem about a true incident of her baby brother and the swan who lived in the river which ran through their garden, and who became extraordinarily tame.

Francis and the Swan

The swans and Francis have lots of fun;
A swan once bit one of his toes.
He did not like it, so he cried.
This was only a small swan, so it did not hurt,
Really.

Another swan taps at our window.
Francis is so very curious,
He snuffles on the window,
And goes S-S-S-S- at the swan.

He thinks he is a swan himself,
And makes such funny noises.
The swan makes funny noises, too,
But the swan does not think he
Is Francis.

Attempts to rhyme were never forbidden, though I was always chary of them, because I had a feeling that the use of both rhythm and rhyme would result in a kind of forced cleverness, or else deteriorate into sheer doggerel. This did, of course, happen now and then, though I must honestly say that I still like both the following examples, doggerel or not.

Tigers

Tigers are so fierce and proud,
They live in the jungle and roar out loud.
They slink through the jungles
Like big stripey mongrels.   (JEFF, 8.)

Pigs

Pigs lie lazily about,
Grunting through their stubby snouts.
Their tails are curly,
Short and whirly,
And they won't get up till you give them a clout.

                    (JILL, 8, inserted in a story.)

Most of the poetry we have produced falls between the high
level of 'Night Hunter' and the doggerel of 'Pigs'. I now give
a representative selection from the last term's work I did in
Kingston, quoting one from every child over seven. Irene's has
been given already, so I start with the next youngest.

To the Robin

Why do you hop on the ground, little robin?
'Tweet. Tweet'.
You dear little robin,
Your tiny red coat might get spoilt.
You will get mud on it, and then—
It will only be brown, like the rest of you.
Why do you do it, my dear little bird?   (NICOLA, 7.)

The Fox

The fox is sly.
He creeps on the chickens,
His glaring eyes are shining bright.
There is a sudden scutter,
And then there is a fight,
And a clicking and a clucking
And a screeching and a squawking,
And the chicken is dead.

But the cruel fox is alive and happy,
As he steals away,
With a good dinner dangling from his mouth.

(MAUREEN, 8.)

The Lamb

My dear lamb, I said,
I want to see how you skip and jump in the fields,
With your snow white coat, and your black tail bobbing
Up and down.
And if you will come to the gate,
I will give you some milk.

But the little lamb took no notice of me, at all.
He just went on skipping. (MARIA, 8; Italian.)

To the Woodpecker

I saw a woodpecker and I said
You are lovely.
You do wrong, though, to nest in a bush;
You live in a tall tree.
I can see that you have chipped away
Half the tree trunk,
But I like to hear you tapping,
All the same. (MICHAEL, 8.)

A Black Insect

O, little black insect, so sweet and pretty,
When you go in the tall-tall grass,
It stands above your little head.
And I am sure it tickles you,
When you creep about under the leaves.

(MICHAEL, 9.)

The Coming of Spring

Spring is in the air.
As she touches the bare branches
The blossoms open,
The green grass waves there

And flowers spring up to see her,
As she walks through the fields.
The birds whistle as she goes by,
The cowslips bow,
Baby birds fly
From their nests so high
And the bees all sing, as she walks their way. (NINA, 10.)

In the Corn

The corn field glows as the wind blows,
Swaying like the branches of a tree.
The corn breaks down
And the little mice, brown,
Make their nests on the ground.   (AVRIL, 10.)

To the Blackbird

O lovely blackbird, sing your song,
At home in your nest is where you belong.
Your babies are crying, so hurry and go:
They are frightened of dangers lurking below.

Your feathers are silky, your beak is so strong,
Your wings are so graceful and your tail is so long.
When the snow lies deep and birds are rare,
Your voice like an angel fills the air.   (JEFFREY, 11.)

The Old Barn

The old barn stands on a hill,
Haunted with mice and memories.
Cobwebs hang from the rotten shafts;
The walls are going to ruin,
And wood worm steals the roof.

The bats take refuge during day,
In this barn, which has beheld so many a story.
And the rats walk stealthily through the ruin,
As the owls peer down from the rafters.

The owl has seen good and bad things.
His mind is a reflection of all that's past;
But soon there will be no more to store,
For the barn is falling to death.   (DEREK, II.)

To the Goldfinch

Flying here, flying there,
Will you never stop?
I want to see your gay bright wings,
And hear you sing.

You hop and hide among the grass,
And cling on the yellow groundsel,
Fluttering in your golden charm
Before the icy winter wind
Blows you far away.   (CYNTHIA, II.)

Water Lilies

The lilies pop open as morning comes near,
The leaves float on water that's crystal clear.
The willows bend over and touch the blooms
Gleaming exotic in watery gloom.

The night draws on and the lilies submerge
Their abundant beauty is lost.
Their sepals close round them like a green ball
They are safe from the cold night frost.   (PHILIP, II.)

I quote one more by Maureen, for a special reason.

Persephone

Among the trees Persephone walks,
And all the leaves turn silver.
They call Persephone, Persephone!
As they sway towards her.
And as she treads upon the grass
The daisies spring out of the ground
Wherever she puts her feet.

The pretty birds sing sweet
And then they cry,
Persephone, Persephone,
Don't leave us any more!

It will not strain the perception of anyone to see that these poems are all related to a single theme in some way. The Persephone poems were written after the middle juniors had been told the story, and had mimed it to the music of 'La Primavera' from the *Concerti delle Stagioni* by Vivaldi, and the bird poems after hearing the second of the concerti, 'L'estate', during a term's work on our own village and all that met our eyes every time we opened the school door.

It is about this kind of approach to work in school that I want to make my final comments before my last chapter, in which I describe the work of one term in detail, and allow the pictures and English to speak for themselves and for each other. The development I have tried to show so far should have made some kind of anticipation of the 'education through the arts' method easy for the reader. From a starting point which was nothing but an intuition that 'art' (meaning drawing) was a good thing, to the realisation that it was an education in itself; to the widening of the field by using art as a means towards a better, fresher view of the social subjects, history, geography, nature study; to the comprehension of its astounding significance in encouraging vital, vigorous, *felt* English, in direct contact with life being lived and to be lived. To bring the wheel full circle, one more turn was necessary. Education must have an end in view, for it is not an end in itself. The end can only be the knowledge of what it means really to live, and the wisdom to accept and make the most of what life offers each individual person. Such knowledge and such wisdom cannot be found within the limits of one's own age, ability and aptitude, nor by heredity, environment, nor instruction. It cannot even be bounded by time itself, for it would be an impercipient spirit who could not 'place' his own inevitable suffering a little better for having read and heard The Book of Job, *King Lear*, or Mozart's G Minor Symphony, and an even poorer one who could not be uplifted by some work of art which for him had special significance.

To believe in their own potentiality for creativity was for the children the first half of their journey towards being educated beings. The other half could be completed only when they could see their own lives surrounded, sustained, and indeed explained by the general experience of all humanity. This part of the journey will take them all the rest of their lives, but to know this is the greatest wisdom they can learn at school. To be able to approach the classic works of art without fear, and with pleasure, interest, understanding and love is to be able to tap the inexhaustible well of past human experience. It was a tentative search for the path leading to the second half of the journey, for a track of some kind that they could in future follow to the world of strength and delight they could find in the arts, that made me recognise the opening when yet another lucky chance delivered the chart right into my hands.

John had been a pupil of the school since he was four, but now he was seven, and about to be transferred to a preparatory school in Cambridge. On the evening of the day he left us, his mother rang me on the telephone, saying that John would like to give the school a present, and could she and John come down to deliver it. Naturally, I was pleased with this mark of appreciation, and as these parents were of the very nicest kind and could be relied upon to choose wisely, I anticipated something in the nature of some really good books for the school library, or something similar. But when John and his mother arrived, I was overwhelmed. The gift was a Pye 'Black Box' record-player!

School had already closed for the Easter holiday, so I kept the precious thing in my house until we opened again for the summer term. On the first morning back I carried it round to school and presented it to the astonished class. After the first dumbfounded moment—I remember only one other like it, when surprise and delight robbed everybody of speech; that was when I announced to them that we had been given the prize for the best co-operative frieze in the 1957 *Sunday Pictorial* Exhibition—the first child to find a voice said, 'Play us something on it'.

I had no suitable records in school, so I dashed round the corner to my house and began to turn over records in frantic haste to find one I thought the children might enjoy. The first one to come to hand was Beethoven's Pastoral Symphony. I rushed back to school and set the disc spinning—no prayers, no register, no dinner money collection, no formal beginning to the day or the term; just twenty-six children, one adult, and Beethoven. At the end of the second movement, Derek said ecstatically 'Isn't it SMASHING!' I felt that it was indeed an extra-special moment, for while they had listened I had found the answer to the problem I had been trying to work out. We were going to base our whole term's work on 'The Pastoral', and see what came of it. The work in the last section of this book is the result.

It was only the first term of several that work was pushed off from some chosen work of art. I called my new method, in fun, 'the symphonic method', but the more I thought about it, the more I realised how apt a title I had hit upon. In this method the separate subjects are analogous to the different sections of an orchestra, playing in concert for full effect every now and then, but in between these moments, first one and then the other taking up the theme. This theme occurs and recurs, but the entire symphony is not one endless repetition of the melody. Though all the work is in some way related to the theme, it is not tied to it nor limited by it, as it is in the so-called 'project method'; nor does it employ one group of instruments only, as in the 'centre of interest' method. My objection to both those otherwise good ideas has been that the various subjects have been made to fit into the chosen theme, whether they would or not, or else neglected entirely because they were too far away to be tied to it, however clumsily. The 'symphonic method' allows for second subjects, bridge passages, variations, differences of tempo and indeed, wholly separate movements; yet the term's work, like a symphony, is only completely satisfactory as an entire whole.

I used this method in planning a term's work on *The Canterbury Tales*. Here, very briefly, is the way it went.

(*a*) I used Elinor Farjeon's translation of the *Prologue* and *Tales*, and read the stories for 'literature' lessons. They were enjoyed immensely, particularly *The Knight's Tale*, which inspired an interest in the literature of romance which never afterwards waned.

(*b*) Passages were used for 'formal' English practice, vocabulary work, comprehension, and grammar. The wealth of imagery in Chaucer, so admirably kept in this translation, was remarked on from the first, and at the end the children were 'collecting' similes and metaphors along with cigarette cards and snail shells.

(*c*) We had a lesson expressly on Chaucer himself, and discussed his description of the Squire from the original.

(*d*) We had a few lessons on the general background of Norman history, leading to the particular period of Henry II, and that we did in a good deal of detail, as the characters of the prologue in turn threw light upon the scene in the court, the church, agriculture, travel, trade, and so on. (I had to stay up late very often, digesting such books as *Social Life in the Early*

Middle Ages, in order to be ready for the questions the next day.)

(*e*) The story of Thomas à Becket and Murder in the Cathedral is always a winner with children. We held a long discussion to decide whether, in our opinion, Becket deserved his fate, and whether Henry gained or lost by Becket's death.

(*f*) The characters and personalities given in the *Prologue* made a deep impression, partly because of the wealth of intimate detail given. Each child chose one of Chaucer's people and made a paper mosaic of him on his horse, as correct in detail as possible, and with much searching of costume and general history reference books. When these were finished, they chose another character, and did a 'close-up'. I told them about medieval manuscripts and showed them reproductions, and they soon caught the idea. They decorated their own pictures with gold paint in lieu of gold leaf, set their close-ups into roundels and covered the surrounding paper with formal leafy 'illumination'. The glowing, broken texture of the paper mosaics gave a most medieval look to the finished works. (At a much later date, I used these and other mosaics in an exhibition which I mounted in our village church as part of a restoration fund effort, hanging them under and between the fifteenth-century originals which are painted on the walls. The comment made by one knowledgeable visitor was that 'the children's pictures looked as if they belonged there'.)

(*g*) 'Singing he was, and fluting all the day.' If the squire could do it, so could they, especially as *The Golden Book of Music* had just come to hand, and they saw from it that there was a distinct relationship between music and manuscript, illumination, the church and life in general. We 'fluted' on our recorders, and sang 'lustily'.

(*h*) Geography looked like being the Cinderella of the term, and I tried, foolishly and of course in vain, to force some kind of interest in maps and so on, by trying to follow, with the aid of Ordnance Survey maps, the route the pilgrims had taken through the Kentish countryside. I need not have worried, for the problem solved itself, as usual.

For free English I set a very broad outline within which they could work to please themselves. They were to write a set of modern tales, one told by each of six characters whom they were to invent from their contemporary social scene. These six characters, we decided, were to meet at London Airport, where a bad fog was to hold them up for a whole night, during which they were to keep each other amused by recounting incidents in which they or people of whom they knew, had been involved.

The problem of what to do for geography did not exist from the moment London Airport was mentioned. The children went to endless trouble to discover the points of departure and the destinations of their modern 'pilgrims', and the stopping places of the world's airlines were soon as well known as those on our own bus route.

The story books themselves were very interesting, both in their own right as stories and as eye-openers to show just how much observation and comment ordinary children are able to bring to bear on the adult world around them. I quote from ten-year-old Derek. In doing so, I have corrected his many, many spelling mistakes, for I see no point at all in celebrating them; but his grammar is exactly as he wrote it. Derek will never be able to spell, I fear, but he can say what he means for all that. I think that every teacher who is honest will agree with me that there is no way that anyone, however clever, can teach a bad speller to spell. If children can spell, they do it from the start; if they can't, it is just too bad—but it is foolish to spend such valuable time as creative English time correcting yesterday's spelling mistakes or writing words ten times each. If you love roses, you do not gain much by cutting off every bud in case they have green-fly. As for spelling

> they will do what they do do,
> And there's no doing anything about it.

Derek's characters were:

(1) An Auctioneer.   (4) A Farmer.
(2) An Army General.   (5) A Professional Gambler.
(3) A Hairdresser.   (6) A Famous Scientist.

The fog grew thicker and thicker until visibility was nil. Suddenly, over the loud speaker, came a woman's voice that said, 'The aeroplane No. 1624 from London to New York is cancelled because of fog.' There was some whispering among the people, and then all was hushed again.

In one corner was a fat man with blue eyes. He was talking as fast as his tongue could wag. He was an auctioneer, who was not very honest. Anyone could see that he was very rich. He bought cheap and sold dear, and made things out to be what they were not, to get more money. He had a big black beard, about six inches long. His hair was thick and bushy. He had all pimples on his face, and several big warts on his chin. He had very thick lips and eye-brows.

By cheating he had got himself a wonderful house which was fit for a duchess to live in, with the most wonderful furniture in it. He had a fleet of seven cars, one for each day of the week. And he never dreamed of going to church. He has money, so he says, 'stored to the roof' in the bank.

He showed off tremendously in front of women. Sometimes he even puts women's make-up on himself.

He always advises people to buy cars which he knows have not got very good engines, but are still very expensive. But for himself, it is just the opposite. He paid his servants appallingly badly. He was not very easy to get on with, either. When he was in a temper, he went as red as a strawberry, and when embarrassed, went as white as a sheet.

I must miss out the descriptions of the other five travellers, but will quote the auctioneer's tale as an example.

I had just bought a house, and moved in. The house was believed to be haunted. I didn't believe it, of course.

One night I heard a scream. I ran downstairs. I saw nothing. So I thought I must have been dreaming. So I went back to bed. In the morning I saw that my wife was not in bed, and I thought about the scream in the night. I shrugged my shoulders, she had probably gone shopping. But it was Saturday, and the shops weren't open. I began to feel uneasy. I began to walk up and down the room. I didn't like it a bit.

At twelve o'clock I knew that something had happened to her. I began to phone the hotels all round the neighbourhood. She wasn't at one of them. I told them all to ring me back if she arrived. The scream kept ringing in my ears. Could it have been my wife who screamed? No, I kept saying, but I searched every place where a murdered woman might be. She was no where.

And then I remembered that there was supposed to be a tunnel in the house. I started to bang on each side of every wall. Suddenly a brick moved and I thought this must be the entrance to the tunnel. I could see that the tunnel had been used not very long before because there was cement dust on the floor. I pulled away more bricks, until I could get through the hole. When I got through, my legs were shaking, I can tell you. At the end of the steps, I suddenly stopped dead. I saw a man leaning over the body of my dead wife. The person heard me and turned and ran. He pushed me out of the way, but I got up and ran after him as he got to the hole he fell over and his skull was smashed open on a brick. I ringed the police up and they said I was to sell the house. So I sold the house and moved away. I got two thousand pounds profit on it, and that is the end of the story.

I have already given a selection from the poems which were part of the term's work on the general theme of life in our village. There are one or two aspects of this term's activities I should like to mention briefly. I am often asked if I have ever found a way of incorporating mathematics into my general scheme of education through the arts. I fear that a truthful answer would be no, not because I could not think of a dozen ways of using mathematical knowledge in the general pattern of what we were doing, but because of the arbitrary nature of the sort of mathematical knowledge that is expected of the children at the top of the primary school. All the incidental work involving calculation of any sort that the children did in association with their other work added to their fundamental understanding of number and measurement, I am sure; but arithmetical processes like compound multiplication of tons, hundredweights, and quarters, were not likely to crop up in the context of the *Canterbury Tales*, though I quite believe some teachers would invent problems of horses and riders crossing bridges that had a weight limit, etc. I feel that this kind of forcing of a round peg into a square hole robs the other work of its joy and spontaneity, and I am against it, unless it rises of its own accord directly out of the matter in hand. In dealing with the village, of course, the boot was on the other foot: we could not have kept mathematics out of it, even if we had wanted to.

We had Ordnance Survey maps covering the district in every size we could get, that is, 1 inch, 2½ inch, 6 inch, and 25 inch maps. From the 6 inch maps we built a contour map of the whole Bourn Valley region, cutting the sections out of plywood and gluing them together. We marked the surrounding villages on it by means of a series of coloured stars which indicated the population of the village at a glance. Every thousand people was represented by a gold star, every five hundred by a silver, and so on. We took a careful census of Kingston itself (we all knew every man, woman and child individually by name, anyway), and this led us to an awareness of all kinds of oddments of knowledge—that the dogs in the village outnumbered the children under eleven by about three to one, for instance.

It took four 25 inch maps to cover the whole parish, and these we pinned down to the school floor. Ordinary steel pins were set upright along the parish boundary at 1 inch intervals.

A strong, fine thread was then stretched round the outside of the pins. This thread was removed and measured, and from it we made a careful calculation of the distance right round the parish boundary. We took tracings of all the farms, and the boys undertook to find out what crop was growing in each field, from which data we were able to calculate percentages of corn crops, root crops, pasture, orchard, etc. The girls tried to discover the ancient field names, and their origins—romantic names like 'Little Winnidow' and self-explanatory ones like 'Bull's Cluss' (Close, of course) and 'Cow's Cluss'. The infants carried out a poultry census, and a domestic animal one, each choosing a kind of bird or animal, and linking it with their other work by writing about it and by making a specimen in crumpled-newspaper sculpture.

We used geometric principles to arrive at a rough guess of the acreage of the parish; we then verified the accuracy or otherwise of our rough calculation by each taking ten fields and adding up the acreage as given, on the 25 inch map, which involved a complete explanation of the decimal system, because all the acreages are given to three decimal places. When each ten fields had been totalled, they were added into a grand total. Mathematics was certainly not left out in the cold this term.

Nor was nature study. Each child tried to discover a different sort of tree growing within the parish. This he studied in detail, and recorded in as many ways as possible. When the trees were in their first glory of new leaf, each did a sketch of his tree and painted it. The sketches were then cut out and mounted together into a panel, which was put together while listening to the Spring Movement from Vivaldi's *Four Seasons Suite*; birds and insects received similar treatment, and wild flowers, observed with great care under a magnifying glass, were then 'blown up' to many times their natural size and a decorative panel made in association with the Vivaldi Summer Movement.

Written English centred round stories in which the children imagined themselves back into history, living in the village when certain little historical events took place. Nicola, aged seven, pretended she was a bat who lived in the church when it was burnt down in 1448; Nina wrote a most touching story of how she was left an orphan by the Black Death; Jeffrey was a village boy who was caught up in the Civil War, and returned to Kingston on the great occasion (I fear legendary rather than historic) when Oliver Cromwell's horse is supposed to have kicked the font over.

The church provided us, one way or another, with most of our history and art work. The culmination was the exhibition of the children's paintings and other pictures hung in the church. The occasion was that of the annual fete for the restoration fund, the church being in urgent need of repair. In passing I must say that all this interest in the church had very little to do with my own allegiance to the Church of England. The children included several from homes where nobody went to any place of worship, several from strongly non-conformist homes, and five Roman Catholics. Kingston has the most delightful, picturesque Congregational Church, which deserves mention in its own right, being made of lath and plaster and thatch, for it was converted from a pair of old cottages. Though interest centred so much on the actual building of the church, we all respected the differences in allegiance to other sects, and discussed them freely. Parents in general were tolerant and most helpful. It was almost as if we had been able to roll back the centuries and see the church as the monument of man's desire to use his heart, mind and hands to the glory of God, and as the natural centre of all the life of the community. Most of the children were christened there, many have already been married there, and some, no doubt, will in time be buried under its walls. This is the pattern of most village churches, but 'my' children can also say that to a large extent they were educated there, as well, like their ancestors back in the Middle Ages.

This was the method used in the work on the Pastoral Symphony, which I hope to describe in greater detail in my last chapter, but there I want the children's essays, poems and pictures to speak mainly for themselves, as all true art should. I must, therefore, add one or two comments in general at this point.

This method is obviously not for everybody, any more than a violin is every musician's instrument; there are many who could get a better tune out of a mouth organ than they ever could out of a violin, and if they know that, they will be wise to leave the violin alone. But have they ever tried anything but a mouth organ? Until they have, they must not be too sure. Then again, for all I know, the sciences, in the hands of an expert teacher, might produce the same amount of interest and the same fresh English. Because I am by nature incapable, it seems, of working up much enthusiasm in myself about scientific matters, I doubt my own ability to teach through the sciences—but I think it could be done, and I expect the results in mathematics by that method would parallel the results I claim for English in my own method through the arts. The real secret of any method is the teacher's devotion and enthusiasm; one string and Paganini makes better music than a bored orchestra and a befuddled conductor. So, if anybody at all in the educational world has enjoyed this description of my experiments enough to start experimenting on his own behalf, I shall be well paid.

Lastly, a word to the specialist English teacher. I have earned, it seems, a small reputation as a lecturer on the teaching of art; but English was my first love and remains my true one. I can, I think, claim to know what real poetry is. I do not accept as 'poetry', even from famous poets, stanzas that simply rhyme faultlessly, or those that scan perfectly, or those that do both and nothing else; I do not accept as 'blank verse' lines that simply conform to 'the five beat thump', and nothing else; least of all can I accept *vers libre* which might just as well, or perhaps better, have been written as prose in the first place. Poetry is a hard thing to define, as many a learned man has discovered. Among our contemporaries, Robert Graves has tried hard to define it, and has not succeeded wholly, but the matter is so near to his heart that he has found a good touchstone, which (for him) is *sincerity*. I add one of my own, for what it is worth, and that is that when a poem says something that could not have been said in any other way, in music, prose, sculpture, movement or paint, then it is poetry.

I know that a great deal of the children's work I have quoted is not 'poetry', but there is, nevertheless, some quality in it that will stand up to my test.

One does not judge children's compositions, as a rule, by comparing them with the prose of Bunyan, for example, or of Lord Chesterfield, or of Hazlitt, or even of Evelyn Waugh; and one should not, therefore, judge Josephine's 'Thanksgiving Hymn' by comparing it with George Herbert's, or Nicola's 'To the Robin' with Keats' 'Ode to a Nightingale'. On the other hand, some of these little poems are 'art' judged by any standard you may apply. I like Beverly's 'Country Sky' better than anything I have ever read by Dylan Thomas, for instance, and Derek's 'Old Barn' better than nine-tenths of Wordsworth's boring descriptive pieces; and when Jill's 'Swan' was included in an anthology, and commented on by a famous critic in a B.B.C. review, I did not think the critic's unrestrained praise a piece of ridiculous exaggeration. But then, these little artists are my friends, and one is always proud to know really creative people; so I am prepared to admit that my pride may have warped my judgement just a little—but I repeat, only a little.

The morning on which I first played the Pastoral Symphony to such new and appreciative ears was a picture-calendar April day, with the sky a glorious technicolour blue (or seeming to be, because for such a long time it had been grey), the clouds wandering aimlessly about it looking more like cotton-wool than clouds, the grass and the new leaves still in their wrapping paper, and the lambs and calves calling to each other across the valley like new toys wound up for the first time. It seemed as if Nature had exaggerated things slightly especially for us, that we might be able to see them better. As soon as I had removed the disc from the player and done the really essential 'first morning back' things, I suggested that we should go out and enjoy the day. I explained that the first movement of the symphony we had just heard was inspired by Beethoven's feelings on first reaching the countryside from the town. They had all known the village from babyhood, but I suggested that they might pretend to see it for the first time.

Cambridgeshire is a flat county, but Kingston does boast a little rise that is grandly called a hill, just on the outskirts of the village proper. To it we went, and gazed and gazed across the valley to the next rise. After the first minute or two, the children needed no more prompting, and as I sat on a five-barred gate and watched them, it was plain to me that they were 'seeing' things for the first time, with every sense other than sight. They tested the breeze, turning this way and that, shutting their eyes and wetting their lips, holding up their handkerchiefs and climbing posts and tree stumps; with closed eyes they explored the texture of grass, tree trunks, gate posts, ditch bottoms, with bare hands and bare feet, laying their cheeks against rugged old elms and pushing little snub noses into clumps of brushwood. They lay flat on their backs and listened, saying to each other, 'Sh! There's a lark' or, 'I can hear a cuckoo so far off I can't hear him', and then opening their eyes again saw the sky above them from a new angle and in new perspective.

Back at school again, we listened once more to Beethoven's first movement while we drank our morning milk, decided to make a co-operative collage of the scene we had seen across the gentle valley, and sat down to record some of our impressions in words.

There were twenty-six children at school that morning, of whom fifteen were seven or more. The remaining eleven, all infants, joined us thereafter wherever we went, and took part in everything except the English work, because most of them were not yet proficient enough at reading and writing to forgo the necessary basic work, though those who could often did attempt to join their seniors in writing up what they had experienced. One of the junior fifteen, an Italian, though he could read and enjoyed doing everything else, steadfastly refused to attempt to write anything or to speak in school, and is therefore not represented in the English examples which follow.

The collage, some 8 feet by 4 feet in size, went forward at every possible opportunity, conjured by excitement and enthusiasm from bits of old cloth, knitting pulled wide apart to show the pattern, straw, raffia, old wallpaper pattern books, lace, silver lamé, cotton-wool, sheep's wool, match-sticks, velvet, hessian. While it was in the making, essays and poems kept abreast of it, on subjects related to it, and there was always the music of the first movement to fall back on whenever we needed refreshment or new inspiration. Many other visits were made to the top of the hill, sometimes by single children, sometimes by little groups. They paid calls on fields of cows, sheep and chickens, and visited birds nesting in the hedges all round us. I cannot possibly give all the work that was produced that term, for it would fill a book by itself; but I shall try to give representative examples of each child's work, both in poetry and prose.

Spring

All birds sing
In the middle of spring.
Flying up in the trees
In the air's sweet breeze.

Then the night will fall
The trees look handsome and tall,
And the owls go silently by,
While the moon hangs up in the sky.

(ANGELO, 10.)

The Sky

The great sky rolls over me when I look up at it. In the far distance, it looks as if it is touching the ground.

There are white and grey-blue clouds and they look very pretty. The white clouds look like a snowball. The blue sky and the grey clouds look very nice together.

The sun looks very beautiful when it is up in the sky with the clouds all round it. At night when it sets, it looks very beautiful indeed.

The sky is very dark at night, but when the stars and the moon are out it looks glittering, bright.

In the morning when you wake up you hear the birds sing in the air.

(STEPHEN, 11.)

Country Sky

The silvery, silky, shimmering clouds float
Daintily in the blue clear sky.
There, in the far distance,
Near the sky-line,
A water-fall of vapour rushes,
Dancing over the silver rocks.
Into a pool of glistening air.

185

Up above, the snow lies crumpled
Into fragments of air.
Then, suddenly—
The pool and the waterfall have gone,
Gone—
Gone for ever,
Never to re-appear.   (BEVERLY, 11.)

In the Country

The wind whistles across the fields of different colours. There are all
sorts of fields: fields where the sheep graze, the field nearly matching
the colour of the sheep: the fruit fields just coming into blossom,
silvery-white: and fields where the green shoots of corn are just
appearing.

Away on the undulating horizon the trees show dark. Some are
almost black, others brown and green. The feeling in the country is so
free, for one can see for miles around.

The sky looks just like a large blue basin, upside down; the clouds
of all different shapes, sizes, and colours float silently into different
patterns. The whole countryside is full of fields, sky, and quietness.

                                                 (JILL, 11.)

Sky

The feathery clouds sail silently by,
Like cotton wool in light blue dye.
On the horizon a heap of snow
Breaks into bits to dance gaily below.

A big black rain cloud comes into sight,
Making the other clouds seem pure white.
The edge of the clouds is dark and grim
Except on those with a silvery rim.   (SARAH, 10.)

In the Country

In the sky you feel a breeze.
As you walk along,
The wind just sweeps across the fields.
As you look,
You see just fields,
With the air that just stretches away.   (AVRIL, 10.)

186

In the Sky

The sky is full of cotton wool,
It is so nice to look at.
It makes a lovely picture,
Whichever way you look at it.

It gives a kind of silver river,
With tiny boats on it.
They are made of gold and silver.
They will soon be out of sight.　　(ROBERT, 8.)

In the Country

The clouds are all white,
The shade dark under trees,
The breeze in the air,
The humming of bees.
The lambs in the field,
The trees waiting about.

The birds are finding little twigs
And feathers for their nests.
The air is all fresh,
The clouds are all shapes,
The cuckoo is about.

Little calves kick up their heels,
And run, because the spring is here.　　(NINA, 9.)

Cows

Cows are very curly on their foreheads. I found the younger ones were much more curly on their heads. The skin was silky on their noses. It seems as if their coats have had a mud bath, especially their legs. They liked the shade very much. Their eyes are soft and silky and they are big and kind and seem to make the whole cow stand out. None of them was the same colour, for they were all different shapes and sizes. Cows are inquisitive. If there is anything on the ground they will come up shyly to it. They never have many calves. They always have very long legs. It is always muddy round the water trough. The tufts on the ends of their tails are mostly black.　　(DEREK, 10.)

Cows

A cow is silky and furry,
He's very nice to look at.
He gives us milk, butter and cheese,
His tummy is fluffy and fat.
I like her very much,
We milk her twice a day.
He is so very nice to touch,
We give him grass and hay.   (ROBERT, 8.)

Cows

The cows' colours are black, white and brown, and some are brown
and white, so that they look like half-baked bread. Cows have big
brown eyes that glare as everybody passes, and round the cows eyes
they have white. Cows have got soft pink noses which are wet, and
they have also got very thin tails which have got like strands of wool
on the ends. Cows have got lovely furry ears, but they are not all fur,
they have pink insides. Cows have smooth fur, but where the dirt is it is
all lumpy; how they get the dirt on their fur is they roll in the mud.
                                                          (CYNTHIA, 10.)

Cows

The skin on cows' necks is rough and when they look round, the skin
moves in waves. Cows have thin tongues, which are for when they
want to eat something they put out their tongue and grab it. Cows'
hooves are just like two front fingers.

   Nearly every cow you see has mud on its fur. They get it by just
simply lying down in the mud. They eat dandelion, hemlock, grass,
leaves, cattle-cake, hay, mangolds, and many more things.
                                                          (JEFFREY, 10.)

Cows

The cows have got lovely woolly coats. Their eyes are all colours.
The nose is an orange colour, and when they drink water, it all goes up
their noses. I like the way they swish the flies off their tails. Their heads
are a very good shape, and their ears suit their heads. It is a funny
mouth, and when they eat grass, they look funny. Cows like grass very
much, and some cows eat and like dandelions. They have very good
manners for when they eat their food.

Some cows are not afraid of you, and some are. When you let cows out, they run very fast, and sometimes it is a long time before you can get them back in proper order. (STEPHEN, II.)

When we had exhausted the possibilities of the first movement, we went on to the second, using the same method. The second movement is perhaps the most 'pictorial' of them all, and the children loved it, identifying the instruments and crowing with delight every time the nightingale trilled or the cuckoo called. We took an afternoon off to visit our little brook, so as to get the feel of it. It was a really warm day, and before long they were all in the brook with dresses tucked up and shoes and socks left on the bank. Some dammed the stream and watched the water as it jumped their barriers, some were content just to squat and trail their fingers in it, some tasted it, others threw stones of different sizes into the water to see the effect, some simply splashed up and down, and others fished with jam jars. The trees hung over thickly, and the whirring of wings every now and then caused dead silence while the bird was located and identified. The cuckoo treated us to a lengthy solo, and we caught a swift glimpse of blue that we hoped was a kingfisher. It was a happy day.

Another collage recorded it for us, done this time as a close-up of the brook and its inhabitants. The cuckoo, the quail and the nightingale of course must be put in; Sarah wanted to include the kingfisher; reeds, flowers, grass, bushes would come as it went along. The music was playing softly while the discussion continued. The 'bit-box' was being ransacked for materials that would suggest other ideas. 'Can I put an otter in?' asked Philip, holding up a piece of moleskin. The record was very near the end of the movement. The nightingale and cuckoo sang their little trills, and the theme wound its way in again. 'That tune's a swan', said Beverly, from the floor. 'I'm going to put a swan in.' I was dubious—swans were becoming a bit

189

of a cliché with us, I felt. I said, 'I don't think Beethoven wrote a swan into it, Bev.' She looked up at me with eyebrows raised nearly to her hairline. 'How *do* you know?' she said. There was no answer to that, so she got her way. Her swan was the most glorious swan ever, carried out completely in white feathers which she and her band of little helpers collected. Jill and Cynthia stitched away with wool and raffia, sewing on doyleys and other fancy papers for flowers and leaves, and a packet of old pheasant feathers covered the grouse and the quail. The cuckoo had to have pigeon feathers painted. We loved every minute of it. The music was better known to us than any in the hit parade, and poems flowed from pens with ease and a sureness of touch that only great joy and complete self-confidence could bring out.

Down by the Brook

The cuckoo flies
And the quail lies
In the broad green grass.
The swan glides along,
And the water sings a song,
While it sparkles like crystal glass.

The weeping willow sighs
As the cuckoo flies
Home as the night draws on.
The nightingale trills,
The sun sets on the hills,
And the light is gone.   (DEREK, 10.)

Down by the Brook

Down by the brook the cuckoo sings
Watching the water running along.
The water bubbles
When stones go rolling along.

The little birds sing to their mothers
As she comes home to the nest,
Down by the brook.   (STEPHEN, II.)

By the Brook

Above the brook the cuckoo sings,
Filling the air with melody.
His mottled breast of yellow and brown
Sweeps over the tree tops,
As he sings his song.
His tail, purple marked with white,
Spreads out like a fan as he flies.

When it is dark the nightingale
Appears from the blossoming trees,
To sing her song, all night long,
Like a little brown elf in the moonlit trees.   (JILL, II.)

Down by the Brook

The rippling brook goes past,
Bubbling over every stone he sees.
The rabbit runs along,
While the cuckoo sings a song.

When you throw a stone, it forms some rings,
When all of a sudden the quail sings.
The quail sings a song,
While the kingfisher darts along.   (ROBERT, 8.)

Down by the Brook

Down by the brook I sat watching the trickling ripples dancing and
leaping over each other. I threw a stone into the water and it immediately jumped over it and looked just like a waterfall.

As a hare ran across the fields I could see his legs prancing, shooting
him across the fields very fast, like an arrow out of a bow.

The cuckoo flies into other birds nests.   (JEFFREY, 10.)

191

Down by the Brook

Down by the brook, the water is shallow and cool, as it bubbles over the stones.

The water ripples and trickles along and it seems as if it is telling a story. When I put my hand in, the water goes over my fingers and looks like a lot of small waterfalls together. When I throw a stone in the water, the ripples go in rings, first into small rings, then into big rings, and they look rather nice. Over the brook, the willow makes moving shadows, and where the willow makes moving shadows, the water is black. (CYNTHIA, 10.)

Down by the Brook

Down by the brook,
The water is running,
and when you put your hand in
the water is cold.
The water runs along the brook.
The rabbit runs about in the field.
The air is fresh,
The water bubbles in the stream,
The stones in the water lie still,
When the water bubbles.
The trees in the shade,
The shades in the water,
The birds in the tree,
In the trees singing. (NINA, 9.)

Down by the Brook

Down by the brook the water goes trippling by. It is nice to watch the water go over the stones. Sometimes wild ducks come down swimming down the water and now and then they put their heads in the water and eat a fish. All kinds of animals and birds come to drink from the silvery coloured water. Fish dart about here and there, and then they dart forward and disappear under a stone.

(ANGELO, $10\frac{1}{2}$.)

Down by the Brook

The kingfisher swoops to catch a fish,
The swan glides along
While a quail sings its song.
The willow weeps
While the nightingale sleeps.
The water runs along
And the cuckoo sings its song.   (PHILIP, 10.)

By the Brook

The water bubbles over the stones
While the wind makes ripples and softly moans.
The water weed is wet and shiny,
Making the bottom smooth and grimy.

A knobbly root sticks out from the side,
On which baby water rats ride.
In the banks are rabbits' holes,
And many others of water voles.   (SARAH, 10.)

Down by the Brook

Down by the brook
The water flows
And sparkles as it gently goes.
Up above the birds fly,
Watching the water trickling by.   (AVRIL, 10.)

Now we came to the third movement, the peasants' merry-making. While we played it through for the first time, feet tapped and fingers ran up and down the desks. It was as though by common consent we had decided how to interpret this movement—by movement. Our village green, just across the road from the school, had in the past been the scene of just such a merrymaking, and would welcome us again. We threw all the windows as wide open as possible, and switched on the record player to its very loudest. The sound carried across perfectly, so we danced. No set movements, just interpretation of the music and the changes of rhythm as they came. After the first once or twice, the spirit of it got into the children's feet. If one half closed one's eyes, one could see the peasants of old, straight from the fields, dancing country fashion just for the love of it.

> Rustically solemn or in rustic laughter
> Lifting heavy feet in clumsy shoes,
> Earth feet, loam feet, lifted in country mirth.

Flushed and breathless the boys threw the girls from one to the other, then whirled away stamping and followed each other round in stamping-rhythm, while the girls stood back to back in the middle of the ring holding their heaving chests and beaming on the circling boys until they were grabbed out again and twirled away into the dance. And all the time Beethoven's music swept across the village from the open windows of the school, while passing motorists looked puzzled from one to the other, as if they hardly believed the evidence of their own senses.

We wanted to make the picture for this movement fit our largest display panel at the end of the school, some 8 feet square. It was too large to 'have about' to be worked on at odd minutes, so we decided that each child, or each pair of children if they preferred it that way, should produce a dancing couple in material (cloth), which should afterwards be cut out and mounted into a composite picture, and the background filled in last. What period of costume? Without thinking, almost, I began to tell them about 'pastoral' poetry, the town man's form of escapism, and the conditions of the real shepherds as history revealed it to be. The picture was forgotten *pro tempore*. We read Spenser, and other 'pastoral' poems; we searched history books for relevant details of rural life. We discovered that shepherd's smocks, by their colour and their patterns, identified the locality from which they came at sheep fairs. I remembered Hardy's lovely poem about the sheep fair in the rain, and we read that. History lived again, no longer caught between the covers of a few text-books on our library shelves. I demonstrated smocking, as well as I knew how, for I am not much of a needlewoman, yet—I hope to improve during my years of retirement; but I had made smocks before and knew how to start, and that was all that was needed. The children soon outstripped me. Rough and crude as their attempts were, they had all the essentials of the making of a smock, and soon their dancing shepherds were arrayed and being matched by girls in print dresses and demure aprons, with plaits made of wool and raffia and binder-twine flying from under their bonnets; our knowledge of puppetry and how to produce quick effects stood us in very good stead. The large picture was soon finished, and the couples danced in a mad gay ring on the painted greensward, while another shepherd played his rural pipe under a tree.

As the couples appeared, they took on characters that were unmistakable, and the children begged to be allowed to write their stories in one of their own books; but time passed so quickly that the idea had to be abandoned, not without considerable regret. We had named some of the little dancing figures, in fun, and the names stuck. I think it was difficult for the children to realise that they were only their own creations, and not ghosts of the real people of the past. The old shepherd playing his pipe came in for a good deal of sympathetic comment, but when Angelo finally placed this figure among the others, he looked surprisingly young, and gave rise to some compositions.

There he sat, under a spreading chestnut tree, a shepherd among his sheep.

The sunlight shone through the branches of the tree, making breaks in the shadows. He sat on the bare grass while his sheep grazed around him. He wore a blue smock, which on back and front was patterned with brilliant colours. The smocking represented roses. His age was about thirty, and he sat thinking.

What could he be thinking of?

Perhaps he was thinking of what he was going to do in future years. Or could he be thinking of what had happened in the past? He may have been thinking that one day he would grow rich, or perhaps of the days when he used to play in the meadows with the other boys. Then as dusk descended, he gathered his sheep together into their pens and walked slowly away to his small cottage.   (JILL, II.)

Of the English work which follows, the most astounding thing to me was the changing rhythms, which had quite obviously been inspired directly by the felt experience of actually dancing to the music. One or two are a bit too clever, with contrived rhymes; once or twice I had to supply a word that rhymed and made sense; but in general these poems were the outpourings of sheer jubilation, controlled and deepened by sympathy for and understanding of the rural past.

A Country Dance at Sunset

The sun is setting in the west,
Dusk is nearly here.
The song-thrush flies home to his nest.
As the evening grows dark, people appear.

Men in their smocks,
Girls in their pretty frocks,
Shepherds with their flocks
Come down from the mountains and rocks.

The people stamp and cheer
To the rhythm and the beat
Of the music so sweet,
While old men drink their beer.

Now the people dance,
Men and women spinning,
Round and round they prance,
Excitement is beginning.

The music is getting faster, faster:
The dancers are swirling.
Now no one is man or master,
For they are all twirling.

But the people depart,
The dance has ended.
When the morning comes
The dance will be—
    only a memory.   (BEVERLY, II.)

The Village Green Dance

On the village green,
There is a dancing scene.
The shepherd plays his pipe,
Underneath the apple tree, with apples red and ripe.

The dancers step so light,
While the sun is shining bright:
The pipers pipe a tune,
In a kind of rustic croon.   (JEFFREY, 10.)

The Peasants Dancing

The earth trembles, as the dancing starts,
A crowd assembles, and they dance with all their hearts.
The prancing shepherds swirl and whirl,
Occasionally glancing at their spinning girl.

The drums bang, and the pipes play,
The dulcimers twang, and the peasants skip and sway;
The big drum booms, the feet thud,
The voices hum, and music tingles in the blood.

A flurried housewife kneels in a ring
Of hurried villagers who dance and sing;
The tune gets slow, at the end of this measure,
And tired people go, to dream of this pleasure.   (SARAH, 10.)

197

The Dance of the Village

The cowmen, the dairymaids,
As well as the shepherds,
Were dancing as well as they could;
And always the piper, a shepherd, would come,
To play a tune on his pipe of old wood.
The sheep would watch,
And the maidens would laugh,
The men would stamp their feet:
As the dancers got more excited,
The little lambs would bleat.
Round and round the dancers twirled,
All the people would shout for joy,
As the maidens' dresses whirled.
So the night drew to a close,
The shepherd stopped his playing,
The people stopped their dancing,
And made way home.
And the moon came out,
Through the cloudy foam.   (JOSEPHINE, 8.)

Peasants' Merrymaking

In the yard,
The thundering footsteps of peasants are heard.
The shepherd sits playing his pipe.
And all the corn is ripe.
The sun is setting in the hill and the dale,
And the sheep seem to wail
As the birds sail
Through the sky.
The people are dancing,
The girls are glancing,
The ladies are prancing;
The sheep are munching,
Green grass they are crunching;
The music is sounded,
They are surrounded
By green leafy dells.

Their feet meet the ground
As they ring the bells,
They twirl round and round,
As the music swells.   (DEREK, 10.)

The Dance

The dancers are spinning round and round,
Their feet do hardly touch the ground.
Some shepherds merrily pipe a tune,
On this summer's day, in June.
The men are dressed in patteren smocks,
The women are wearing pale mauve frocks.
The music changes beat,
And weights the rhythm of the dancing feet.   (JILL, 11.)

The Merrymaking of the Peasants

On the village green,
Peasant girls are seen,
Dancing very gay,
In among the hay.

The shepherd plays his pipe.
The men are very polite.
The girls are twirling,
And the men are swirling.

To another shepherd's song.
O, what a happy village throng.   (PHILIP, 10.)

The Dancing

As the workmen were dancing,
As the shepherds were glancing,
The maidens were prancing along.
And all the wives were dancing,
And one of the shepherds was playing,
A pipe made of wood.
The maids were dancing in their aprons,
The men had big black boots.
The maidens' buckles shine in the sun,
For they had shoes with buckles on.   (NINA, 9.)

The Dance

As I was walking along the village green, I saw the shepherds and cow-maids dancing round and round. The men were dressed in smocks, and the maidens dressed in frocks. The shepherds were dressed in smocks and the maids were dressed in frocks. The shepherds played their pipes and some sang as they played. The shepherds and maids kicked up their legs and again as they went round and round.

The cowmaids danced with the shepherds and looked gay going up and down with a shepherd playing his pipe in the middle.

When night fell they left their dancing and went away into the distance.

(STEPHEN, 11.)

The Dance

On a green, peasants were heard, dancing. At first it was very light, and then it came to heavy dancing. In the background, trees were waving and the birds were singing a song.

The shepherds played the pipe while they danced on.

The young girls had full dresses, with white aprons and hats. The girls' shoes were made of leather, and the buckles shone in the sun. The girls' feet were dainty ones, which kicked up in the air, as the music played.

(AVRIL, 10.)

The Country Dance

As I was walking down the road to see a country dance, I saw that the people who were going to dance were not there.

I waited a while, and to my astonishment there they were, young and old shepherds, each with a maiden by his side, holding hands. Suddenly I remembered, that these were the people of long, long ago.

They all started to dance, round, round, up, and down they all went together.

The first piece of music was merry and light, but after a little while it became heavier, and louder than ever: then a merry tune came in again, which was a young shepherd playing his pipe, under a spreading oak tree. All the people twirled round and round, and kicked their legs up, and then they went off in a long line, and I knew that the dance had ended.

(ANGELO, 10.)

On the village green sat a shepherd playing his pipe. Around him danced some young peasant girls, with young and old peasants.

The dancers first danced lightly and then the tune changed and the dancers began to dance heavily. The young peasant girls wore a full skirt sewn on to a bodice; they also wore a little white cap and a little white apron. The shepherds wore a smock with coloured patterns on and some trousers under their smocks. Up above, the birds sang and fluttered to the pipers music. The trees in the background made a gentle breeze, while the dancers danced happily.   (CYNTHIA, 10.)

As any one who is familiar with 'The Pastoral' will know, there is no break between the merrymaking movement and the storm. And so it proved, for on the Friday afternoon on which we finished the large picture of the dancing, and hung it proudly at the end of the school, the sky, which had been practically cloudless for a month, suddenly grew heavy and lowering, and the children were sent home early to avoid the coming storm. They had, however, had the whole of the second side of our record played to them that afternoon, and had listened to the orchestral storm with interest. They went off under the black skies without the least sign of fear, but remarking how the church stood out against the darkness, and how the trees bent in the sudden wind. The storm did not come that afternoon, and during the sunny evening several disgruntled children came to my gate to complain that they hadn't had a chance to see it, after all. They need not have worried, for the Saturday evening brought the worst storm of the year, a whole night of violence and brilliance to which no orchestra or paint brush could ever do justice. Monday morning brought the children back at school filled with the experience of watching and listening to nature's roarings. 'I got out of bed and watched it for a long time', said one. 'Mummy was frightened, but I wasn't', said another. 'I kept thinking how we could make a picture of it.' 'I woke up and was scared, so I put my head under the bedclothes and tried to write a poem.' 'There's a piece of gold string in the bit-bag that would make a lovely flash of lightning', etc.

The storm scene shows Kingston in the grip of the storm, with the church and several cottages produced accurately as to detail, and the aforesaid string one vivid flash of lightning above all, in the dark, windswept sky. For some reason which only they knew, by common consent they wrote their descriptions of the storm in prose. Perhaps they felt that their poetry could not do justice to the spectacle, and thought it safer not to try.

The Thunder Storm

The day had been very hot, and towards evening, thunder could be heard. It rumbled in the distance, and gradually came nearer.

Everywhere grew dark, but all of a sudden a flash of lightning lit up the room, then the thunder crashed, then it trundled across the sky as though a trolley was being pulled about. Then all was quiet except for the rain beating on the ground and the window pane.

Water ran down the road, and from the roofs of houses. In the darkness of the storm, the trees looked dull, but the ground was nice and fresh. All the grass was heavy with rain.

But now the thunder began to die away, and the lightning was not so brilliant. The storm was gone, and all was quiet.   (JILL, 11.)

It is thundering and lightening gigantically over the little village. All the people are very frightened. The light is dimmed by the clouds; some of them are peculiar shapes, some like fish and other things.

The trees sway about like the mast of a ship, and the wind whines like a gale in winter. The roads are silent as the thunder storm goes on. The lightning is like golden streaks across the sky, forked lightning as well as sheet.

The sky is gradually getting clearer and the people are coming out to see if the storm had gone, and it has almost stopped raining and the wind has dropped and it is fine again.   (PHILIP, 10.)

The thunder roared, the lightning crashed and the trees swayed as the wind rushed through their branches.

Through the houses leapt the lightning, with thunder in the air; nobody cared to walk outside, when the rain was teaming down and everything wet through and dripping puddles on the road. The grass was now sopping and swaying hardly at all, because of the rain weighing it down.

Dirt ground was now mud, fields were swimming, and ditches full to the brim.

The rain was getting slower, the thunder was going away into the distance, and the lightning was no more. (JOSEPHINE, 8.)

The thunder rolls across the black, inky sky, softly at first, then growing to a deafening roar, which makes the very earth tremble.

Flash. A streak of lightning zigzags, brightening up every swaying tree. Shadows appear, making frightening visions. A mother passes with two children huddling against her skirt. They stared with big wide eyes at the dark trees towering over them. A dog lies cowering under a small bush, where it whines at the whistling wind.

Crash. An uprooted tree leans drunkenly against a sturdy oak. In the houses, people shudder and dive under the bedclothes hardly daring to breathe. They peep out like timid mice to blink at the thunderstorm. (BEVERLY, 11.)

It was a very hot afternoon with the sun shining down on everything. Then when the evening came, the sky turned from the beautiful blue to a dark, menacing black. Then in the distance you could hear thunder rumbling through the sky.

You could hear it come closer, and then streaks of lightning flashed through the trees and houses, making them all tremble. Then the rain started to come down, fast and faster it came. It seemed as if it was snowing, because you couldn't see through it, and trees were pulled right out of the ground. The wind whistled through the trees.

After the rain had all left off, everywhere you looked everything was flooded, even some of the houses. You could only see the roofs and the chimneys.

The night fell softly, and the storm was over. (ANGELO, 10.)

The lightning streaks and flashes across the sky, shaking trees and sometimes striking them down. You can actually see the streaks of forked
lightning in the sky.

The deafening, crashing thunder rumbles through the sky, and then
—flash. The lightning springs again like a wild yellow beast. Then you
can see the blackish dark blue, and you can smell the thunder.

Then it happens; the rain comes pelting down, making brooks high
and cornfields flat. As the rain pours down, the rushing winds blow
the raindrops down towards each other, like a wall of rain as it beats on
the ground and then suddenly the rain dies off, and you can hear it
going away.   (JEFFREY, 10.)

The rain splashed on to the window sills of every house that lay
beneath the storm. The thunder rumbled in the distance, making a
peculiar noise, which turns into an unbearable roar. People in bed
draw their blankets closer and try not to see the blinding flashes of
lightning. The animals huddle together in frightened groups with
mothers trying to protect their cowering babies.

The wind howls through the dripping trees; in bed, people shudder
at the thought of being out in such a deluge. Far away, a dog's whine is
mingled in another crash of thunder. Newly planted trees are uprooted,
and as another crash of thunder and flash of lightening criss-crosses the
sky, a gnarled oak is struck by lightning, and will forever have a
burned inside.

The zig-zag of lightning brightens up the rolling black thunder
clouds from which the torrents of rain are coming. As the wind
blows the trees sway from side to side making ghostly shapes that
frighten any human being that happens to see them. Water rats in their
flooded holes stare at the thunderstorm and wonder what the meaning
of their soaking is. But when the storm is ended, the river drops and
they soon forget the storm.   (SARAH, 10.)

The thunder crashed through the air, as the lightning lightened the
trees. The people dart here and there to get into their houses.

The shapes of the clouds are ghostly to look at. The wind makes a
horrible sound in the air as the rain falls.   (ROBERT, 8.)

The storm had aroused a good deal of speculation as to which
instruments were doing what noises. At this point we made a

study of the orchestra, painting and cutting out the players and their instruments, so as to show them in their right places, and learning a few simple facts about each section of the orchestra as we proceeded. While we were about it, we studied the life of Beethoven, and learned the very simplest of facts about symphonic form. The following composition is Sarah's, who had already got into the habit of writing things down to make herself remember them better—a good thing for her, perhaps, as she was one of the two children in this batch to get a grammar school place.

The Symphony and Beethoven

A symphony is a composition of music written for a whole orchestra with no soloist. Until about 1800 a symphony was generally for only two people, but since then many symphonies have been written and nowadays as many as a hundred people play them. A symphony for two would not be called a symphony any more.

Symphonies are made up of four movements, (with the exception of Beethoven's Pastoral Symphony, which I think is the only one ever to have five). The first movement is generally quite fast. It is made up of two themes which keep coming in again and again, woven in and out, and the development. The second is slow and quiet, and more difficult to play. The third movement is a Minuet and Trio, because the rich people listening used to get tired of sitting still after the first two movements and liked to get up and dance to the third. The fourth is again quick and lively.

Many composers wrote symphonies. Ludwig van Beethoven was just one of them. He was born at Bonn, in Germany. He was always fond of music. At Vienna he had some lessons from Mozart, who told him that there was very little he could teach him.

Beethoven had always been rather ugly, but when he was about twenty-five he got a kind of blotchy rash on him, which made him look terrible. He wrote nine symphonies, of which the Pastoral is the sixth.

No one can say that this method does not lead to a store of general knowledge! We had reached the last movement, with the thanksgiving hymn and then the haunting little theme tune. The children were getting a bit tired of paint and collage, and unanimously voted that the thanksgiving picture should be left in the hands of Angelo, whom they considered to be the best artist among them. Luckily Angelo was pleased with this commission, and set off for the church all by himself, where he spent a whole morning sketching the screen and other bits of architecture that he wanted in his picture. He took the rest of the term to complete the fifth picture, using his playtimes and lunch hours as well as all the time I could possibly allow him to have away from his normal studies in school. He reproduced the screen with black paper and a pair of scissors, in exquisite detail, and a stained glass window, which our church has not got, came out of his head. Meanwhile, every child had written a thanksgiving hymn.

Thanksgiving Hymn

Now the storm is over,
And all of us are glad.
We thank thee Lord, for safety
In the awful storm we had.

The thunder claps have gone away,
They filled us all with sorrow;
We hope that we may dance again
Upon the green tomorrow.   (JILL, 11.)

The thunder claps have finished,
And the lightning has diminished:
O, Lord, we had a lot of fear,
But knew that you were near.

The sun is shining bright,
We are no longer filled with fright.
Although the sky is bright and clear,
We all know that you are *still* near.   (PHILIP, 10.)

206

Gracious Lord, you have saved us all,
Grown-ups and children, big and small.

Help us, Lord, to fear it not again,
The thunder storm, with lightning flash and rain.

The thunder is gone now, and nobody fears:
Help us to praise you, Lord, all through the years.

(JEFFREY, 10.)

God, the father of all men,
You have saved us once again;
Now listen while we praise you here,
For helping us in storm and fear. (ANGELO, 10.)

Lord, we were in thunder and rain,
But now we are safe and warm again.

The wind tore our hair, and made our eyes smart;
But now there is gratitude in each person's heart.

The brooks overflowed their sodden banks,
Now to thee we give our grateful thanks.

You have saved our children and wives;
We shall be thankful all our lives.

Across the black sky, thunder roared;
For our safety in danger, we thank thee, Lord.

(BEVERLY, 11.)

We thank you for saving us from the wind,
When the thunder crashed,
And the rain splashed,
And the lightening flashed.
To thee we sing praises for being so kind.

The big trees swept and swayed,
When the thunder growled:
Like a wild beast it prowled,
While the wind howled,
And on the ground little trees it laid.

Now we are here our thanks to give.
The sky and clouds were rent,
But when you came, the thunder went.
Thank you for your mercies sent.
We will not forget you, as long as we live. (SARAH, 10.)

Holy Father, You are near,
And have saved me from this fear.
Now, good Father, I am here,
My song of praise to sing so clear:
Help me now to love you dear.   (JOSEPHINE, 8.)

This might have been the end. But there was that little tune, so singable, and tappable, so whistle-able that we all went round humming it and singing it and whistling it all day. We studied it as a piece of music, tapping the rhythm, learning the notes and the time. With the help of my daughter, more musical than I, we transposed it so that we could play it on our recorders. Then I asked for the last piece of work of the term in English. I talked for a few minutes about the symphony they all now knew so well, saying that we had really spent a musical day out in the country. We had arrived in the morning, spent the afternoon by the brook, attended a dance on the green in the evening, from which we had been forced to take shelter in the church during the storm, and where we had joined in the evening hymn of praise for our safety. Now the country people would all be going home, in different ways, to different places, with different thoughts in their minds and different feelings in their hearts. What I wanted them to do now was to go home from the church with one of the villagers, in spirit; and to write an 'end-of-the-day' song, *the words of which would fit the tune.*

I must say that the children looked aghast at this awful task, and for a moment or two, I really thought I had overstepped the limit and asked the impossible. But they squared their shoulders, sucked their pencils, and set about it. By sheer instinct, they chose to write lullabies and love songs. The boys wrote the lullabies, the girls the love songs, though it might perhaps have been expected the other way about. Angelo wrote just an 'evening song'.

Evening Song

The dancing is over,
The people go back home.
For now night is coming,
And only lovers roam.

But early next morning,
The sun will shine out bright;
The men will stroll down to the fields,
All in the morning light.

Jeffrey and Philip wrote lullabies.

Pastoral Lullaby

To sleep now, to sleep now,
My pretty baby dear,
To sleep now, to sleep now,
And dream away from fear.

It's morning, it's morning,
The sun is rising high;
The bells ring, the birds sing,
My darling, please don't cry.   (JEFFREY, 10.)

The Shepherds' Lullaby

It's evening, it's evening,
The light is growing dim,
Your cradle is rocking,
We've sung our evening hymn.

The stars are shining,
The moon is rising high;
My darling, my darling,
The night is drawing nigh.   (PHILIP, 11.)

Sarah and Jill wrote love songs.

> My sweet heart, my sweetheart,
> The dancing now is over.
> Come walking, come talking,
> Among the trees, my lover.
>
> The sun's gone, the moon's come
> But I will walk with you.
> Along the lane, we'll stroll again,
> All in the evening dew.   (SARAH, 10.)

This was good, but for sheer success, I hand the palm to Jill, who caught, in this, her last poem in the school, for she was due for transfer, the complete simplicity, the integrity, the forthrightness of country love. When I picked up her poem and sang it, I experienced a moment of exhilarating success and a conviction that my efforts had not been in vain.

Love Song

> My darling, my darling,
> Oh, will you be my wife?
> I'll care for you, I'll share with you,
> And love you all my life.
>
> My sweetheart, my sweetheart,
> Of course I'll marry you:
> I'll cook for you, I'll wash for you,
> And I will love you true.
>
> I'm sure we'll be happy,
> You need not fear, or sorrow.
> So kiss me, don't miss me,
> I'll ask your dad to-morrow.

By this time most of the younger children had given up trying, the task being truly a bit too great for them; but Beverly was still deep in puzzled thought, and as she was usually the one to be relied on, it was strange that she was having such difficulty. At last she spoke.

'I simply can't write an end-of-the-day one', she said. 'But there's another poem that keeps wanting to come about the symphony all together.' 'Then write the one that wants to come', I said. After a few minutes, she passed up to me the last poem I am going to quote, one in which she, perhaps, has summed up the term's work for me better than I could ever have done it for myself.

Symphony

The music is slowing,
It's drawing to an end,
The rhythm is flowing,
The weaving tunes still blend.

The oboes were singing,
They made a pretty air:
The violins were stringing,
The double bass was there.

The flutes, bassoons, and piccaloes
In harmony agree,
And all the swelling music goes
To make the symphony.

The symphony is over, now. The giant, Progress, has removed the disc from the player, and closed the lid; for in the name of Progress, aided by his henchmen Economy and Expediency, the school has been closed.

The first official intimation of the impending doom reached me at a social function connected with another school when it was publicly announced that my school, along with that of one of my oldest and dearest friends, who was sitting beside me, was to be closed. My friend and I played our parts for the rest of the afternoon, pretending we did not care, but tears could not be long delayed. I had known, of course, from the time I had first taken over the school, eighteen years before, that it had been scheduled for closure ultimately, and I was not naïve enough to think that any new growth or fresh flowering of a school (other than that represented by numbers on roll) would influence the impersonal, rate-controlled machinery of local government to spare any tree once marked for felling. All my foreknowledge did very little to soften the blow when at last it fell so rudely.

I felt as a sculptor might feel to see his creation toppled from its pedestal and smashed, a painter to watch his canvas ripped, or an author to know his manuscript had been burned. I grieved for the village I had grown to love so much, for I felt that it would die from the day its heart was torn out. In numbers it may grow again as the spread of new houses from Cambridge reaches it, but a dormitory housing estate is not the same thing as a self-contained village community, and in any case the green will no longer echo to children's voices, nor 'a joyful noise unto the Lord' be heard floating across it from the open windows of the school.

I had some concern for myself, too, wondering what the future could hold that was half so precious and exciting as the past. I had no fear that I would not get another post, especially if I cared to leave the county, for I had been offered the chance of such places on several occasions. The prospect did not please me, however, because I wanted something that could make up to me all that I was losing, and this a 'better' job with more salary and greater prestige alone could not do. Half-heartedly I applied for two posts in the vicinity, but it was as I had suspected: it remains as true as ever that a prophet findeth no honour in his own country, and the local managers did not want me. To add to my general depression I became ill, and was told that an operation was the only solution. The future did indeed look bleak.

Then from between the thunder clouds I caught sight of the first glimpse of blue sky again, in the form of an idea which, though laid aside for a long time, had never been lost or forgotten. For six years I had been attending a university tutorial class on literature held at Bassingbourn Village College under the auspices of the Board of Extra-Mural Studies of the University of Cambridge, and I had been told that every year they offered one or two bursaries to mature students to enable them to read for a degree at Cambridge. I was more than what is usually meant by 'mature', at least as far as years were concerned. I knew that I was probably over their age limit, but I had to make the attempt. I wrote a long essay on 'The Decline of Rural Idiom and its Effect on Literature', filled in an application form, sent them off with only twelve hours to spare before the closing date, and like Piglet when he had thrown his 'missage' into the flood, I knew I had done all I could to save myself, and retired into hospital for the operation. A month later, having been out of hospital thirty-six hours, I faced the selection board at a 'short-list' interview. For nearly thirty years I had stood just outside the doors of the University, but they had opened to me at last. One of New Hall's few and precious places was offered to me, and the dream of my life had come true.

The children and I spent one last term together, making the most of everything and learning to accept the inevitable, looking forward to the future with hope and courage even in the same breath as we regretted the joys of the past. As Shakespeare said,

Welcome ever smiles, but farewell goes out sighing.

I hope the children won't forget, any more than I shall. They have passed on to schools which are much larger units, with undoubted advantages in most aspects of education. It does, however, still depend on what is meant by that poor overworked word. If I 'educated' the children in my care at

213

Kingston at all, it was, I hope, to help them to enjoy life. Whatever kind of education they get in future, no one will ever be able to take *that* away from the particular little group who lived through the 'pastoral' term with me in my little school. A true music lover does not need to have the score always before him, nor to keep a record of it continually playing; he can carry the whole symphony for ever in his head.

NOTES

ON THE

PLATES

1 Jeffrey (9). *Vase of flowers.* Paper mosaic, 24 by 24 inches.

2 Beverly (11). *Isaiah, ch. 11, v. 6.* Paint, 40 by 30 inches.

'The wolf also shall dwell with the lamb, and the leopard shall lie down with the kid; and the calf and the young lion and the fatling together; and a little child shall lead them.'

A beautiful example of the inspiration one art can be to another. The picture was the response to the emotion felt at meeting the words for the first time, as Beverly sat dipping here and there into a beautiful bible given to us by the Trustees of the Todd Charity, for the use of teacher and children alike.

3(a) John (4½). *Pattern.* Paint, 20 by 15 inches (page 112).

A typical example of the pattern which so often emerges from the first scribblings or daubings with paint; perhaps a schematic human figure.

3(b) Philip (4½). *I've drawed a tree.* Paint, 14½ by 12½ inches (page 113).

Chance movements of the brush have produced a pattern resembling an object already well known and named. In recognising and naming the object in his picture the child has made the first step towards understanding pictorial representation. This is also a significant step in his general education because modern reading schemes, etc., use pictures as introductory agents on the supposition that children understand them, a premise not to be relied upon in a great many cases.

4(a) Charlie (4½). *My family.* Paint, 20 by 15 inches (page 60).

4(b) Maureen (6). *Daniel in the lions' den.* Paint, 20 by 18 inches.

Only one lion is complete with a body; to a child of six, as to the poor victim thrown to the lions, the heads are the significant features.

5(a) June (5½). *Trees.* Paint, 22 by 15 inches.

A strange but beautiful picture in scarlet and crimson by a nervous, tentative child retarded by ill health. She was delighted, not only with the pattern and colour of her creation, but with her success in producing a picture recognisable by the other children. It was a great event in June's short time with us.

5(b) Irene (5). *The angry witch.* Paint, 19 by 12 inches.

A very young attempt at recording emotion. There is no doubt that this witch merits the epithet the child applied to her, and as Irene announced before she began the picture what she was going to paint, this may be accepted as a genuine case of thought and feeling communicated by a five-year-old's skill with a brush.

6(a) Matthew (5¾). *Witch* (No. 1). Wax crayon, 20 by 12 inches.

6(b) Matthew (5¾). *Witch* (No. 2). Paint, 20 by 12 inches.

7(a) Matthew (5¾). *Witch* (No. 3). Paint, 20 by 12 inches.

7(b) Matthew (5¾). *Witch* (No. 4). Paint, 20 by 12 inches.

8(a) Matthew (5¾). *Witch* (No. 5). Paint, 20 by 12 inches.

A whole art education in fifteen minutes; Matthew had previously refused to attempt any form of picture making.

8(b) Matthew (5 10/12). *Trees in the wind.* Paint, 25 by 20 inches.

The strength and vigour of these scarlet and black trees against their blue sugar paper background show what enormous confidence the incident of the witch pictures, only three weeks or so previously, had given Matthew. From this picture on, there was no stopping him.

9 Matthew (6). *With a comb and a glass in her hand.* Paint and gold ink, 25 by 20 inches.

10(a) Irene (5½). *Hens in our garden.* Wax crayon on cover paper.

An 'odd-minute' picture. The hens are coloured mainly in black and white, with 'Freart' crayon laid thick on soft green cover paper. One or two of the largest birds in the centre have bright orange and scarlet breasts.

10(b) Mark (6). *There's a chicken on the wall.* Paint and wax crayon, 20 by 18 inches.

This was painted immediately after the children had listened to the B.B.C. programme called 'The Music Box', in which they had been invited to sing the words 'There's a chicken on the wall' to a piece of music. Note the strong effect of the wax crayon patterns on top of very free painting, and the quick but effective filling of the background by a wax crayon used on its side.

11(a) Roger (7½). *Cow and calf.* Paint, 17½ by 14 inches.

A loving, truthful record of a delightful scene observed with the seeing eye of an animal lover before leaving for school that same morning.

11(b) Jennifer (9). *Cat among the crocuses.* Paint, 20 by 20 inches.

A straightforward illustration of a little poem found in a library book.

> In the crocus bed I saw her,
> Like a queen enthroned she sat;
> Yellow crocuses shone round her,
> Royal, sun-illumined CAT.

A marmalade cat with green eyes and a white waistcoat among yellow crocuses on soft green pastel paper.

12 Jill (6). *Portrait of Mrs Marshall doing her requisition.* Paint, 25 by 20 inches.

To see ourselves as others see us! An unsolicited record of what a poor teacher looks and feels like when trying to get a whole year's supplies out of £30. The first of Jill's surprising masterpieces, which also include the poem 'Swan' and the love duet set to the last little theme of the Pastoral Symphony.

13 Roger (7). *My family.* Paint, 25 by 20 inches (page 60).

14(a) Angelo (10). *Tiger.* Paint, 25 by 20 inches (page 115).

14(b) Philip (10). *Tiger.* Paint, 25 by 14 inches (page 115).

15(a)   Roger (9). *Lady arranging flowers*. Paint, 20 by 25 inches.

From what depths of Roger's mind this picture came I cannot guess. It was done in an art lesson, from the title given to the whole class. All the other children's pictures were ordinary women standing arranging very English flowers. It is difficult to believe that Roger was the son of a labourer living at an isolated farm, and that as far as I know he had never seen a Japanese print. I questioned him as closely as I dare to discover what had prompted his picture, but he seemed to have no idea of what it was that had given him this idea.

15(b)   Jean (11). *Tea in a cafe*. Paint, 20 by 18 inches.

One of the very few pictures I have which show the shift of emphasis from pleasure taken in the actual execution of the picture to pleasure stimulated by the subject-matter—a natural development about the age of puberty. The complete freedom with which Jean had always previously painted gave way, in this picture, before a desire to explore in paint the delights of adult life as she imagined them; that is, to wear a hat with a veil, to smoke a cigarette, to chat with a friend over tea in a cafe, and to be waited on by a waitress in a white cap and apron.

16   Gay (8½). *St Hugh of Lincoln*. Paper mosaic, 20 by 15 inches (page 85).

17   David (8). *St Bernard*. Paper mosaic, 20 by 15 inches.

David had little skill in his fingers and did not enjoy picture making with paint and crayon. This was the first paper mosaic he ever attempted, and the result, in the most subtle shades of browns, greys and white, broken only by a brilliant yellowy-orange setting sun, was a revelation to me of the enormous sensitivity and artistic potentiality of the boy, whose failure until this moment had been caused by the fact that he was not in sympathy with the media he had been offered.

18   Josephine (9). *Incident at Upway*. Paint, 20 by 23 inches.

An illustration of Hardy's ironic little poem about the encounter between a handcuffed convict and a small travelling fiddler on a station platform.

19   Roger (11). *The Crucifixion*. Paper mosaic, 30 by 40 inches (page 62).

20 Angelo (11). '*A merchant was there with a forked beard.*' Paper mosaic, 30 by 20 inches.

21 Cynthia (10). *Orion watching the Pleiades dance.* Paint, 30 by 20 inches.

22 *The Last Supper.* Paint, 57 by 36 inches.

One of a series of pictures telling the story of Christ's passion. For this set the children worked in small groups, each group being led by one of the older children. This group consisted of Cynthia, eleven, in charge, helped by Philip, eleven, Josephine, nine, and Michael, eight. The other pictures in the set measured 8 by 4 feet, except the crucifixion, which was 6 feet square.

23 Jeffrey (10). *Harvest Festival.* Paint with wax crayon, 30 by 20 inches.

24 Derek (10½). *The Wife of Bath.* Paper mosaic with a border pattern of gold and red paint, 26 by 26 inches.

The wife's hat is of black felt and her cuffs are oddments of Victorian braid from the bit-box.

25 Jeffrey (11). *Thirteenth-century soldiers.* Paper mosaic, 25 by 25 inches.

Imaginative reconstruction of the thirteenth-century wall-painting in the chancel of the church. Note the difference in the pattern of the chain-mail on the legs of the two soldiers, observed and reproduced with great exactitude from the faint reddish brown outlines left, after six centuries, on the chancel wall.

26 Derek (11). *St George and the Dragon.* Paper mosaic, 30 by 30 inches.

Reconstruction of a fifteenth-century wall-painting, even more indistinct and incomplete than the soldiers, from the nave of the church.

27 Derek (11). *Page from illustrated version of Psalm 104.* Pen drawing and ink wash (page 158).

'The young lions roar after their prey, and seek their meat from God.'

28(a) Cynthia (11). *Psalm 104.* Picture for 29 (a). 15 by 10 inches.

28(b) Jeffrey (11). *Psalm 104.* Text page for 29 (b). 15 by 10 inches.

29(a) Cynthia (11). *Psalm 104*. Text for 28 (a). 15 by 10 inches.

29(b) Jeffrey (11). *Psalm 104*. Picture for 28 (b). 15 by 10 inches.

30(a) Irene (7). Picture for 31 (a). Pen drawing with wax crayon. 15 by 10 inches.

30(b) Jill (9). Page from an illustrated version of the poem 'Fancy', by John Keats. 11 by 10 inches.

31(a) Irene (7). Text for 30 (a). 15 by 10 inches.

31(b) Jill (9). Picture for 30 (b). Ink drawing and wash of water colour.

32(a) Jennifer (9½). *And to the young ravens which cry*. 9 by 7 inches. A page from Psalm 147.

An interesting point of technique in this little picture: it is done by overlaying one thick wax picture with another. The top layer is then scratched with a sharp instrument (in this case an old pen nib), to allow the under layer to show through.

32(b) Carol (9½). *Roman figures*. Charcoal with paint. 7 by 9½ inches.

An illustration from our village history book.

33 Co-operative. The second (slow) movement of the Pastoral Symphony, 'By the Brook'.

The whole picture measures 8 by 4 feet, and the approximate size of the swan is 36 by 24 inches.

34 Beverly (10). A dancing couple from the co-operative picture illustrating the third movement of the Pastoral Symphony, 'The Peasants' Merrymaking'.

The whole panel measures 8 feet 6 inches square; this couple is approximately 24 inches square. It is made of cloth, leather, old nylon stockings, fur, lace, binder-twine, etc.

35 Co-operative. *Storm over Kingston*. The fourth movement of the Pastoral Symphony, 6 by 3 feet. Paint, cardboard, gold string, straw, cellophane, net, lace, etc.

36 Angelo (10). End page of a free story-book called 'The Adventures of Long-Ears'. 11½ by 8 inches.

Wax crayon on rough orange cover paper.

THE PLATES

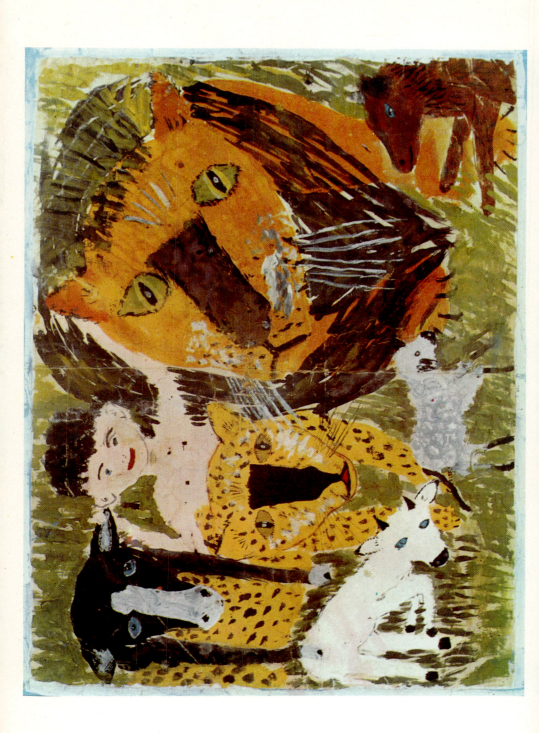

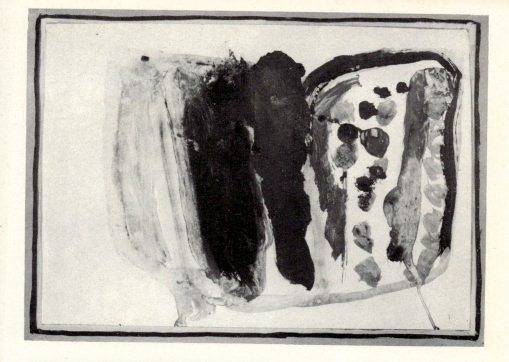

3 (a) JOHN 4½
  (b) PHILIP 4½

4 (a)   CHARLIE 4½

(b)   MAUREEN 6

5 (a)   JUNE 5½
   (b)   IRENE 5

6 (a)   MATTHEW 5¾
  (b)   MATTHEW 5¾

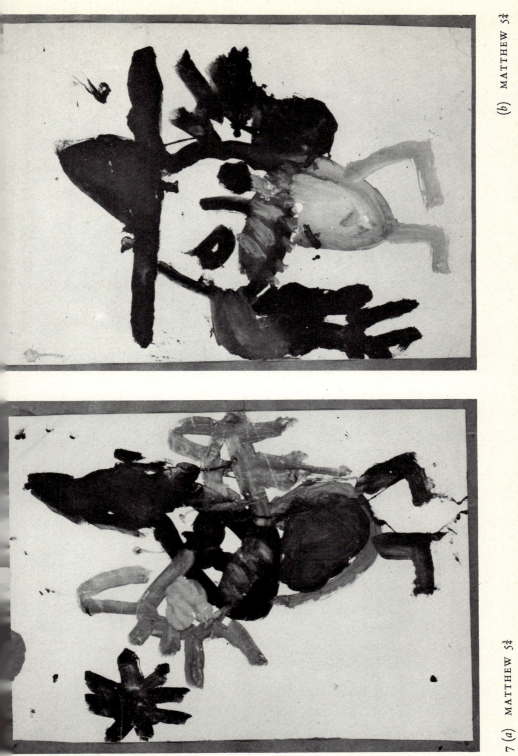

7 (a) MATTHEW 5¾   (b) MATTHEW 5¾

8 (a) MATTHEW 5¾
  (b) MATTHEW 5 10/12

9   MATTHEW 6

10 (*a*) IRENE 5½
   (*b*) MARK 6

II (a)   ROGER 7½
   (b)   JENNIFER 9

13 ROGER 7

14 (*a*) ANGELO 10
(*b*) PHILIP 10

15 (a) ROGER 9
    (b) JEAN 11

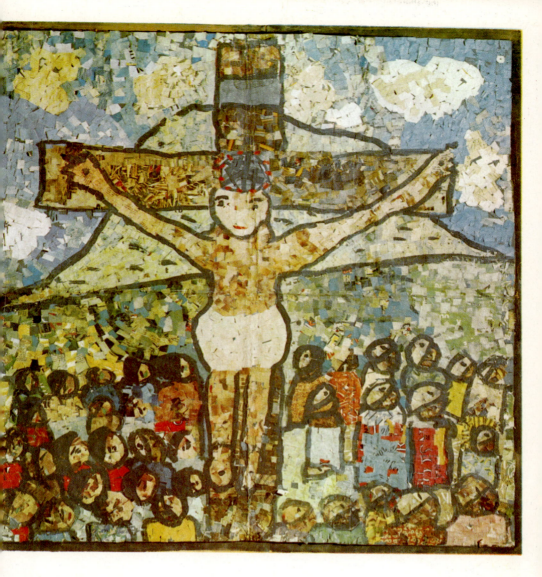

26 DEREK 10½

27 DEREK II

So is this great and wide sea, wherein are creeping innumerable, both small and great beasts.

28 (a) CYNTHIA II
   (b) JEFFREY II

29 (a) CYNTHIA II
(b) JEFFREY II

All the buds and bells of May
From dewy swarl or thorny spray.

30 (a) IRENE 7
(b) JILL 9

By them shall the fowls of the
heaven have their
habitation,
Which sing among the
branches

31 (a)   IRENE 7
   (b)   JILL 9

32 (a) JENNIFER 9½
    (b) CAROL 9½

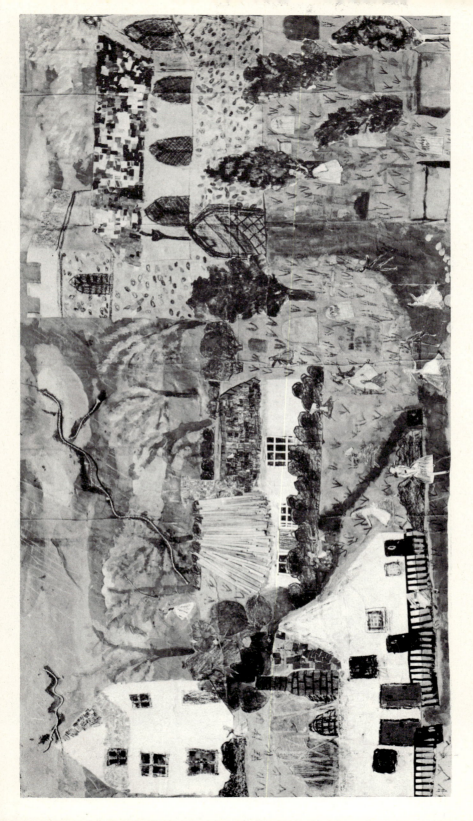

35 CO-OPERATIVE